DRAMA AND THE WHOLE CURRICULUM

Edited by Jon Nixon

HUTCHINSON

London Melbourne Sydney Auckland Johannesburg

Hutchinson & Co. (Publishers) Ltd

An imprint of the Hutchinson Publishing Group

17–21 Conway Street, London W1P 6JD

Hutchinson Group (Australia) Pty Ltd
30–32 Cremorne Street, Richmond South, Victoria 3121
PO Box 151, Broadway, New South Wales 2007

Hutchinson Group (NZ) Ltd
32–34 View Road, PO Box 40–086, Glenfield, Auckland 10

Hutchinson Group (SA) (Pty) Ltd
PO Box 337, Bergvlei 2012, South Africa

First published 1982

Set in VIP Plantin
by D. P. Media Limited, Hitchin, Hertfordshire

Printed in Great Britain
by The Anchor Press Ltd
and bound by Wm Brendon & Son Ltd,
both of Tiptree, Essex

British Library Cataloguing in Publication Data

Drama and the whole curriculum.
  1. Drama in education
  I. Nixon, Jon
  371.3'32   PN3171

ISBN 0 09 149251 3

DRAMA
AND THE WHOLE
CURRICULUM

'97

1397

Contents

PART THREE: WIDER CONTEXTS

Preface and acknowledgements

The idea of this book was conceived while I was teaching at Woodberry Down School. It would have been still-born were it not for the constant frustrations and occasional excitements of trying to fulfil the duties of head of drama within that institution. My thanks are due to those students and colleagues who helped create the necessary context of discontent.

I should also like to acknowledge my debt to Margaret Nixon and Jean Rudduck, who commented on a paper which was to form the basis of the editorial introduction, and to Geoffrey Hodson for advice on the project at various stages of completion. Raymond Verrier's willingness to discuss editorial doubts and dilemmas has, as always, been invaluable.

My debt to Lawrence Stenhouse is incalculable. Almost single-handed he has created an intellectual climate in which practitioners can achieve articulacy in the field of curriculum theory. If this symposium contributes to a grounded theory of educational practice, it is due very largely to his influence.

Jon Nixon
Middlesex Polytechnic
October, 1981

The contributors

Gavin Bolton has been at the University of Durham as specialist lecturer in drama in education since 1964. He has served on many national committees and was one of the assessors of the Schools Council Drama Teaching Project (10–16). His major publication is *Towards a Theory of Drama in Education*, 1979.

Leslie Button is Senior Lecturer in Education at the University College of Swansea. He is the author of *Discovery and Experience*, 1971, *Developmental Group Work with Adolescents*, 1974, and *Group Tutoring for the Form Teacher*, 1981. He is also the director of the Action Research Project in Developmental Group Work.

Ken Byron is Teacher Adviser for Drama in Leicestershire. Previously he taught English and drama in secondary schools and was lecturer in drama at Hamilton College of Education. He edits *2D*, an international journal for drama and dance in education, and has written a number of articles on drama teaching.

Peter Chilver is Head of English at Langdon School, East Ham. He is co-author, with Gerard Gould, of *Learning and Language in the Classroom: Discursive Teaching and Writing Across the Curriculum*, 1982.

Elyse Dodgson has worked in theatre in the USA and Britain. She is Head of Drama at Vauxhall Manor School and is currently researching the experience of West Indian women in Britain as part of a school focused in-service education project. The purpose of this project is to develop materials for use throughout the curriculum.

9

John Fines is Head of History at the West Sussex Institute of Higher Education. He is currently Deputy President of the Historical Association. He has written widely on history and on the teaching of history. His major academic publication is the *Biographical Register of Early English Protestants*, 1981.

Terry Jones is Drama Adviser in Devon. He is also a General Secondary Adviser and Pastoral Adviser to a group of primary schools. He has twice been Chairman of the National Association of Drama Advisers.

Barbara Lanning is a Senior Lecturer in English and Drama at the West London Institute of Higher Education. She is a regular guest lecturer on ADB (Ed.) courses in London and a member of the London District WEA tutors' panel. Since its inception in 1978, she has led the Drama Workshops for the Blind in Harrow.

Jon Nixon is a Senior Lecturer in Education at Middlesex Polytechnic. Until recently he was Head of Drama at Woodberry Down School, North London. He has edited *A Teacher's Guide to Action Research*, Grant McIntyre, 1981.

Pam Schweitzer is an education worker with Task Force. She also works as a lecturer on theatre-in-education and deviser of educational materials for use in schools and colleges. Previously she has taught drama in schools and colleges and worked as a drama advisory teacher. She has edited three volumes of theatre-in-education shows, Methuen, 1980.

Julian Watson is Head Teacher at Castlecroft Primary School, Wolverhampton. He has worked in four other primary schools and lectured in drama, movement, and education at Worcester College of Higher Education.

Introduction: The debate within educational drama

Jon Nixon

There have been two basic approaches to questions concerning the purpose of drama in schools. The first has been largely theoretical. It has developed from theories of art and culture and from recent studies in developmental psychology. The work of Susanne Langer, for example, which was largely inspired by Ernst Cassirer's earlier philosophical investigations into the meaning of symbolic form, has trailed in its wake a shoal of books and articles attempting to define what is unique to educational drama. Jerome Bruner's insights into the 'enactive mode' as a crucial phase in the development of the child's understanding of the world have also occasioned some interesting, if rarefied, speculations.

The second approach has been empirical rather than theoretical. It has concentrated on the minutiae of classroom transactions. The innumerable decisions made by a teacher in the course of any lesson have undergone detailed analyses aimed at discerning patterns of teacherly response. Since the work of the 'new sociologists' has so obviously informed this empirical tradition, the sociological naïvety which underpins it is somewhat ironic. Viewed through the lens of transactional analysis the classroom is often reduced to a grid of codes encapsulated from the harsh realities of school and society.

Although offering some useful insights, neither of these two approaches has proved adequate to the needs of teachers using drama in schools. For many of the problems encountered in the classroom are a direct result of the narrow view taken by schools of the relation between drama and the whole curriculum. Such problems cannot be solved solely by the formulation of clearer definitions or the development of more appropriate teaching skills. A third approach is needed

11

whereby teachers are helped to explore the cross-curricular function of drama.

This book sets out to define the parameters of such an approach. It looks at how the curriculum finds its way into the classroom and at how the concerns of the classroom are in turn reflected in the broad organizational structures of the school. It is a book for the cosmopolitan of the curriculum; for the teacher of any discipline who is committed to forging creative links between subjects and working collaboratively on the design of new syllabuses and courses.

Precisely because the book is addressed to a wide readership this introduction covers some familiar territory. Those who have travelled this way before might well move directly to the opening section. However, those less conversant with the terms of the debate might find it useful to review some of the issues which have shaped thinking within educational drama over the last thirty years.

The need for a theoretical framework

The Department of Education and Science Survey, *Drama* (1967), while championing the cause of drama in schools, adopted a cautious stance:

The claim that drama can contribute to self-discovery, personal and emotional development, and human relationships, has been substantiated by much of the admirable work we have seen and the testimony of many heads. But a good deal of the work going on in schools does not live up to the claims that are made for it. [DES 1967, p. 107]

Reservations voiced by the author of the Survey continued to find expression in much of the subsequent writing on educational drama.

The Bullock Report in 1975, for example, acknowledged 'the value and high quality' of much of the drama in schools, while at the same time contending that in most schools it had yet to realize its potential 'in helping the child to communicate with others, to express his own feelings and thoughts, and to gain confidence in a variety of contexts'. (DES 1975, p. 161). It was a sad reflection upon the state of drama in education that after a span of eight years the Bullock Committee still needed to point out the failure of drama to fulfil many of the claims made for it.

More radically, *Schools Council Working Paper 54* asked whether these claims themselves were educationally sound. Published in the same year as *The Bullock Report*, this paper drew upon the findings of the Arts and the Adolescent Project which ran between 1968 and 1972. In the paper Malcolm Ross, the project organizer, tried to show that many arts teachers were confused as to their function within the educational system, and that many of their claims were defensive rather than expressive of any real understanding. 'When asked about their aims and their understanding of their own educational function,' commented Ross, 'most of the arts teachers I spoke to were either struck totally dumb or rapidly collapsed into incoherence.' (Ross 1975, p. 17)

The critical note struck by Ross chimed in well with the opinions of two drama specialists working in higher education. David Clegg, in a hard-hitting and highly personal article, maintained that 'drama teachers at all levels behave as if they didn't want anyone to check on what happens – as if they were scared that someone might eventually call their bluff'. (Clegg 1973, p. 38) Discussing what he termed 'five fallacies in drama', John Pick took up a similar position. Drama teachers, he claimed, all too frequently 'siphon off any query about purposes into that great sedge of platitude which passes for educational discussion'. (Pick 1973, p. 6)

Implicit in this somewhat gloomy view was the urge towards greater clarity among drama specialists concerning the purpose of drama in schools. One County Adviser for English and drama responded to the remarks of Pick and Clegg by suggesting that drama teachers tended to operate a restricted language code which denied them the opportunity of developing an effective rationale for drama in schools. What was needed, he argued, was 'a well-wrought philosophy' which would give confidence and articulacy to those many teachers who felt that drama was worthwhile, but who needed greater support in knowing 'just why it deserves and demands a place in the curriculum in its own right'. (Lloyd-Evans 1974, p. 80)

It was largely in response to this dearth of theory that in 1974 the Schools Council set up a three-year project to consider the aims and objectives of drama teaching in the 10 to 16 age range. Its further brief was to find possible ways of assessing outcomes and to suggest ways in which drama could be organized in the curriculum. The project team

---

* For full references see the Bibliography at the end of this book.

worked with six local education authorities across England. In each area three schools were selected and classes in each school observed over a year so that development could be noted. In addition, working parties were organized in each area to consider the place of drama in the curriculum.

The team developed a conceptual framework by means of which the range of drama work they had observed could be analysed. Within this framework the drama process was defined in terms of four components:

Social interaction   Drama is essentially social. As children participate they are encouraged to interact on both real and symbolic levels.

Content   Drama revolves around problems, questions and issues of understanding. The content of drama is united in that it is seen at the level of human behaviour and interpersonal response.

Forms of expression   As participants explore problems of meaning and understanding through drama they are experimenting with different ways of representing them through the roles and situations they devise.

Use of the media – the 'language' of drama   The way in which content is explored and the forms of representation which are discovered and used are affected by the participants developing skills in the media of drama. [McGregor *et al.* 1977, p. 23–4]

These components were in turn related to four main areas of learning: learning to use the process; understanding themes, topics and issues; participating in presentation; and the interpretation and appreciation of dramatic statements by other people. (McGregor *et al.* 1977, p. 25) By formulating this conceptual map the project team hoped to provide a basis for considering the ways in which aims and intentions can be translated into practice. It was in its analysis of classroom practice, however, that the final report was least successful. Case studies produced by the team lacked detail and were rarely checked against either teachers' or pupils' accounts of what had taken place in the lessons. As for providing a means whereby teachers of drama could develop a method of systematically evaluating their own practice, the project barely made a start. It was precisely because of this failure to explore the practical implications of its own framework that the project unwittingly marked a significant turning point in the debate: away from a preoccupation with theory for its own sake towards the question of what kind of theoretical framework would best suit the needs of practising teachers.

This was the question which Gavin Bolton addressed in *Towards a Theory of Drama in Education*. The book was an advance upon that produced by the Schools Council Drama Teaching Project team, not only because of the economy and clarity of the framework it offered, but because it represented a genuine attempt to further the emergence of a theory that would be firmly grounded in classroom practice. His starting point was his own varied experience as a teacher of drama:

I want to confine myself here to what theories may be drawn from a certain kind of contemporary practice. . . . Most of the examples of practice will be drawn from my own teaching – the good *and* the bad. Sometimes it is easier to make a theoretical point from one's mistakes, especially where those mistakes go beyond mere errors of judgement to wrong or misunderstood principles. [Bolton 1979, pp. 1–2]

If we accept as general the possibility of making 'a theoretical point from one's mistakes', then Bolton's argument implies that all teachers can become their own theory builders.

Seen as a response to those earlier calls for a serviceable theoretical framework for drama, Bolton's work presents us with something of a paradox. For it is at once the theoretical statement many people claimed to have been waiting for and at the same time an intelligent denial of the possibility of producing any single theoretical statement applicable to every classroom. *Towards a Theory of Drama in Education* stands, as its title suggests, as a marker pointing the way towards the kind of theory to which practising teachers might make a unique contribution.

The drama *versus* theatre issue

The supposed distinction between drama as a process of learning and theatre as an end-product is a commonplace in discussions among drama specialists. The extreme positions in the debate were firmly stated in an exchange which took place between John Crompton and Ken Byron. Briefly, Crompton set out '. . . a progression of "activities", each dramatic, involving increasing complexity, physical and intellectual, from the simplest mimes and movements to the most difficult acting and stage techniques.' (Crompton 1973, p. 145) Ken Byron rejected Crompton's suggestions on the grounds that they were based upon theatre-biased thinking, treating drama as a body of

15

knowledge rather than as a process of learning. 'I cannot accept one particle of this approach', insisted Byron, 'because it seems to me that the essence of real drama work is to find out *where the children (or adults) are* and to work from there.' (Byron 1974, p. 29)

That key phrase of Byron's was a curious echo of Brian Way's oft quoted 'begin from where you are'. (Way 1967, p. 28) The influential and widely read book in which that phrase occurred was to provide a rallying point for drama teachers throughout the late 1960s and early 1970s. The tradition on which Brian Way drew had taken root, however, some twenty years earlier. It was in conferences such as the one held at the Bonnington Hotel in 1948 that Peter Slade established the dichotomy between theatre and educational drama as an issue which was to inform much of the discussion concerning the place of drama in schools for the next thirty years.

A participant at that conference has since recalled how, while there, he realized for the first time the depth of the split developing between the concept of drama in schools and that of the theatre arts. 'It is a distinction that I still am quite unable to accept', he has remarked, 'though it appears to exist wherever in the English-speaking world new attitudes to drama in schools have taken root'. (Allen 1979, p. 12) John Allen is not alone in having rejected a distinction which is now widely considered to be, if not entirely false, at least based upon a somewhat simplistic conceptual model.

Those whose knowledge of Dorothy Heathcote's work is largely by hearsay, and who see her as having inherited the mantle of Peter Slade, may be surprised to find in a major study of her work a chapter headed 'theatre elements as tools' and opening with the following statement:

Classroom drama uses the elements of the art of theatre. . . . The difference between theatre and classroom drama is that in theatre everything is contrived so that the audience gets the kicks. In the classroom, the participants get the kicks. However, the tools are the same: the elements of theatre craft. [Wagner 1977, p. 147]

Anyone who has observed Heathcote in the classroom will know that as she sets up the drama work she relies on her theatrical sense.

Gavin Bolton's work reveals a similar willingness to incorporate the elements of theatre into the child's experience of drama. Starting from the assumption that 'depth of learning is likely to take place when the

16

experience is structured in a way that simultaneously meets the requirements of the educational objectives and of the art form', (Bolton 1977, p. 3) Bolton reaffirms the central importance of the concept of 'showing' in any pedagogy of classroom drama. He also sees, however, and spells out the danger of, an exclusive reliance upon performance-oriented drama: 'pupils never experience . . . ; they simply demonstrate what they already know'. (Bolton 1977, p. 101)

In 1979 the wheel seemed to have come full circle with a conference organized by Gerald Chapman and John Dale, directors of the Young People's Theatre Scheme at the Royal Court, and funded by the Greater London Arts Association. Unlike the Bonnington conference of thirty years earlier, the purpose of the Riverside conference was to span the 'widening abyss between educational drama and the various aspects of the professional theatre'. (Robinson 1980, p. 1) Participants included theatre directors, teachers, actors, educational advisers and actor/teachers, who were invited to contribute any observation about the nature of theatre and educational drama which might suggest an important relationship between the arts and education in general. Although there was heated division on a number of issues, the conference did help to give greater credibility to the idea that drama and theatre may achieve a common focus within the classroom.

One issue highlighted at the conference was the need for drama specialists to think more clearly about the political implications of their own teaching. The theatre, it was argued, had learned to approach social issues in material terms. Drama teachers, on the other hand, still tended to rely upon subjective experience. It was only when their analyses of social problems was informed by facts and figures culled from books, pamphlets and newspapers, suggested Nicholas Wright, that pupils could begin to study the mystifying effects of ideology and to decide for themselves whether these problems were in fact problems at all, and, if so, what could be done about them. (Wright 1980, pp. 88–104)

Wright's forestalling of any easy consensus concerning the relation between drama and theatre was timely. For the arguments advanced by Heathcote, Bolton and others can all too easily blind us to the fact that, although perhaps philosophically untenable, the supposed distinction between drama and theatre has entered the folklore of the teaching profession. As such it still determines the way in which many drama specialists perceive their work in schools.

17

The subject *versus* method issue

At a conference of the Drama Sub-Committee of the Schools Council English Committee, held at Lady Margaret Hall, Oxford, in 1972, participants yielded a wealth of opposing views on the question of whether drama should be seen as a subject or as a teaching method:

Drama is not a subject. (It is) a medium through which children develop.

It is essential that drama be used as a separate subject area in its own right.

It was suggested that drama was not a subject but rather a tool or an activity in the same way that writing is. [Schools Council 1972]

The degree of uncertainty on this issue led to a recommendation for a project to be set up by the Schools Council to look at various curriculum models for drama in schools.

In the event, the publication five years later of the report of the Drama Teaching Project (10–16) did little to dispel the sense of uncertainty. Having limited their discussion of the place of drama in the curriculum to a brief outline of the workings of block release and the modular timetable, the project team concluded the single chapter it had devoted to the subject with the bland assertion that, provided a school has clear aims and objectives in introducing drama into the curriculum, 'it is possible, fairly simply, to devise timetable structures which will facilitate the achievement of those objectives and repay their investment'. (McGregor *et al*. 1977, p. 188) It was left to Her Majesty's Inspectorate, in a paper which gave the lie to that telling phrase, 'fairly simply', to discuss, albeit briefly and without specific reference to drama, what form such 'timetable structures' might take. (DES 1977, pp. 78–84)

The decision by the project team to address itself in the main to questions of pedagogy could be seen as yet another instance of the broader curriculum issues being shelved in the interests of survival. Many drama teachers in secondary schools felt they had enough trouble establishing drama as a respectable activity in its own right, without pursuing the additional problem of offering drama as a service to other subject departments. They preferred, as an Australian observer pointed out, 'to pursue the service aspect of drama from a position of subject strength rather than from one of subject weakness'. (Deverall 1975, p. 7) A broad base of support existed for the notion of drama as a subject in its own right, not only from those who rejected 'the service aspect of drama', but also from those who, although favouring it in principle, chose for tactical reasons to adopt 'a position of subject strength'. There were, however, those for whom the advantages of tactical compromise held little attraction. One of the clearest expressions of this viewpoint has come from Geoff Gillham, director of the Cockpit Theatre-in-Education team in London:

> I do not consider drama as a subject in the sense that mathematics or geography is usually thought of. Rather, I consider it a skill or tool for teaching about other things. It is more analogous to audio-visual aids, or maths-blocks than to maths. It is there to be *used*, when it is appropriate to do so, not to be timetabled for half an hour a week at the end of a day.   [Gillham 1977, p. 106]

Gillham proceeded to outline an integrated project-based curriculum which he developed while working as an advisory teacher in Newcastle-upon-Tyne.

This project was not without precedent. Several Schools Council projects had employed drama as a teaching method in the development of curricula. In particular the Social Studies, Integrated Studies and Moral Education Projects had all utilized drama techniques such as simulation and role-play to a substantial degree.

Arguably, a case for using drama as a teaching method across the curriculum was implicit in the traditional association between English and drama. This association was based on the fact that within both these curriculum categories there was concern for the spoken language and with the study, appreciation and creation of dramatic literature. The Anglo-American Seminar on the Teaching of English, held at Dartmouth College in 1966, reaffirmed this vital link. 'What we are recommending', wrote Douglas Barnes in one of the six monographs published as a result of the conference, '. . . is not only that drama activities be part of all English teaching, but that all English teaching approach the condition of drama'. (Barnes 1968) At the heart of this recommendation was the belief that teachers should direct attention more and more to the child's active engagement with the text and away from the purely academic study of literature and language.

Another relationship that has received some attention is the one between drama and history. Once again there is a traditional association between the two. In the past, however, this association has tended to be one in which history is seen simply as a source of drama material and drama as a way of presenting fact through historical pageant.

The work of John Fines and Raymond Verrier, working from the history department of the former Bishop Otter College, Chichester, represented a radical break with the tradition of scripted and unscripted playmaking based on actual historical events. Reacting against the kind of teaching which, they felt, reduced history to the 'mindless conning of more and more dead information', (Fines and Verrier 1974, p. 83) they developed a team-teaching approach which, through the use of improvised drama, accorded greater value to children's own statements and actions. The co-operative style of teaching demanded compromises on either side. The specialist historian of the team 'had to put away content and his deep respect for inviolate truthful facts', while the drama specialist 'had to spend long hours of reading and research, building for himself an armory of facts' (Fines and Verrier 1974, p. 9). But the gains for the pupils in terms of historical learning and understanding were considerable. For what was being developed, claimed Fines and Verrier, was the 'ability to feel what others felt – the power of empathy' (Fines and Verrier 1974, p. 89).

There are, nevertheless, those who argue that even if drama could be made to work in other subject areas it should still be seen as a subject in its own right. John Allen has stated categorically that 'to claim that drama generally is a tool for teaching other subjects is an offence to Shakespeare and a disservice to the very specialists who are making the claim' (Allen 1979, p. 75). Underlying the rhetoric is Allen's firmly held belief that drama possesses its own body of knowledge, which he locates here within the field of dramatic literature, and that as a result drama deserves a slot of its own on the timetable.

The state of drama in schools

The lack of a united and coherent voice raised on behalf of educational drama over the last three decades has meant that drama teachers have been slow to develop an effective power-base within schools. This state of affairs has had several unfortunate consequences for those working in the field of educational drama.

The analysis of a Department of Education and Science national sample undertaken by the School Council's Arts and the Adolescent Project (Ross 1975, pp. 31–45) showed that insufficient provision had been made in the secondary school curriculum for drama. Curriculum allocation in secondary modern schools during the year 1965/6 was 1 per cent, while in grammar and comprehensive schools in the same year drama constituted still less – half of 1 per cent of the curriculum. Moreover, although total provision for the arts during the first three years at comprehensive school was 12 per cent, during years four and five this figure dropped to 9 per cent. Clearly, drama was considered unnecessary both for the academically able and for the older child.

The national sample also showed that the professional standing of drama teachers was in many cases less secure than that of teachers from other subject specialisms. Most of the drama teachers had qualifications which were recognized not as straightforward degrees but as degree equivalents. Furthermore, the arts subjects in general relied more than other subjects upon assistance from part-time staff (10 per cent of all arts teachers were part-timers against 5 per cent of language and 3 per cent of science teachers). The fact that only 5 per cent of headteachers had studied any of the arts subjects confirms the suspicion that there was a low ceiling in the career prospects of drama teachers.

Similar findings were reported in a more recent survey of 259 secondary schools (Robinson 1975). Ken Robinson, a member of the Schools Council Drama Teaching Project team, found that in his sample a fifth of those teaching drama had received no drama training. Most of the teachers who had been trained to teach drama came from colleges of education. Of these specialists, 42 per cent took the subject there as a main course and over half of those who took drama as a subsidiary course took it in a college of education. There were very few graduates.

A final and perhaps more damaging consequence of the insecure position of drama in schools is the isolation in which many drama teachers have been obliged to work. In Robinson's sample 40 per cent of the specialist teachers were found to work alone. Moreover, only sixteen of the 294 teachers who taught drama did so for the whole week. Most specialists taught it for less than twenty hours a week and many taught more English than drama. Professional links between teachers of drama were therefore difficult to maintain.

The attitude of many teachers to the state of drama in schools has recently found expression in the call for a national pressure group which would concentrate the lobby for drama teaching in schools. Traditionally, drama teachers have been represented by a number of professional associations, each serving different interest groups: the

British Children's Theatre Association, the Educational· Drama Association and the Society for the Teachers of Speech and Drama. However, at a conference attended by more than a hundred drama teachers, and held at the Cockpit Theatre in 1976, participants expressed concern that none of these associations adequately represented those working in schools. They claimed that teachers had no voice on the recently constituted Drama and Theatre Educational Council (DATEC), which advises on the professional training of actors and the study of drama at universities, colleges of education and polytechnics, and proposed the creation of a new body to be called the National Association for the Teaching of Drama (NATD), which would apply for membership of DATEC.

Perhaps in response to this and similar criticisms, the 18-year-old British Children's Theatre Association, on 5 January 1977, renamed itself the National Association for Drama in Education and Children's Theatre (NADECT). As the editor of the Association's journal pointed out, 'the new name was devised to show that we are concerned equally with children's theatre and with teachers in the classroom using drama as a method of education' (Porter 1977, p. 3). In defiance of the proposal put forward at the Cockpit Theatre conference the previous year, he claimed that with its committee of practising experts in separate fields NADECT was a truly national body with very powerful grass roots.

Despite the efforts of NADECT to win popular support, the NATD was formed in 1977. Within two years it claimed to represent 1500 teachers and have links with a hundred education authorities. It stated its primary objectives as being 'to improve the status and development of drama teaching at local levels' and to 'co-ordinate and disseminate information and formulate policies at national level' (NATD 1979).

At its annual conference, held at York University in January 1979, the NATD produced a statement on the needs and requirements of drama teaching. It called for more specialist drama teachers with better career opportunities, the appointment of specialist drama advisers in all local authorities, a greater share of the timetable and better facilities. Adequate in-service training was particularly important for drama because of the practical nature of the work, the statement emphasized (NATD 1979). It would seem that the NATD may go some way towards providing drama teachers with a sense of professional solidarity which hitherto many seem to have lacked.

One of the consequences of this increased security has been a greater willingness on behalf of NATD members to see themselves as agents of curriculum change. A recommendation from one of the discussion groups at the second annual conference, held at Queen's College, Oxford, in March 1980, read as follows:

Curriculum changes ultimately come from the actions of teachers in schools, while external factors exert only a limited influence. We need to concentrate on the maintenance and development of Drama and the Creative Arts in our own institutions and not expect radical change to be effected from without. [NATD 1980]

It looks very much as if the teacher members of the NATD are beginning to respond – in their own way and at their own pace – to those calls for a serviceable theoretical framework which characterized the debate within drama circles during the early 1970s.

The present study must be seen, therefore, as part of a general urge among drama teachers to develop a grounded theory of educational practice. It explores, at precise points and within specific sectors, the relation between drama and the curriculum as a whole. The content of the book should be self-evident. Part One raises a number of curricular issues and provides principles and procedures for exploring these issues in specific settings. Part Two focuses on the classroom and looks at a number of examples of work carried out on the frontiers of drama – in the context of language studies, the teaching of social issues, history and the arts. Finally, three contributors look to the wider educational context in order to document a number of agencies which can be used to support curriculum development within drama.

No definitive statements are offered in the following pages; no simple solutions to problems which by their very nature are complex and uncertain. The suggestions put forward are provisional. They are intended as springboards rather than landing mats. The reader should take those ideas that seem applicable to his or her own situation and develop them accordingly. The rest may well be left to colleagues working under circumstances perhaps more conducive to change. One of the marks of effective curriculum development at the local level is its capacity for operating within the constraints and inconsistencies of a system it seeks to modify.

One word more. The fact that we are here arguing a case for the cross-curricular function of drama in schools does not mean that we in any way minimize the status of 'drama as a discipline of thought'★. Drama is a bounded game of conventions, not just a matter of personal development; an occasion as well as a continuum. It is precisely because drama is a distinct mode of understanding which tells its tale through the representation of human behaviour that it has a vital part to play in the whole curriculum. For there is no area of learning which does not relate in some way to how we behave as human beings.

★ The title of a talk given by Professor Lawrence Stenhouse at the third annual conference of the NATD held at the University of Keele, April 1981.

PART ONE

Curriculum Structures

1 Philosophical perspectives on drama and the curriculum

Gavin Bolton

It has always been a headache deciding how, when and where to place drama on the school curriculum. The decisions seem to depend on locating its position at the intersection of three perspectives:

1 As assumption about education and knowledge.
2 An assumption about the status of the subject.
3 An assumption about the status of the teacher.

The headache has often been brought on either because one or more of these basic assumptions remains unclear or because they have seemed incompatible.

However I recently came across an example of straightforward coherence among the three perspectives. This was an instance of a teacher appointed to a senior high school in USA who was appointed to be responsible for the school productions. In this case, the assumption about education was that of the behavioural modification tradition; the assumption about the status of the knowledge was invested in the importance of performance skills in acting, stage-dancing and singing (the repertoire seemed to vary from rock musicals to the more 'classical' *Oklahoma*); and the status of the teacher was that of trainer and director. A parallel to be found in the UK, which matches the American example in straightforwardness but is even more circumscribed in its intentions, is the case where a teacher passes on to his pupils information about the history of the theatre so that the pupil can regurgitate those facts in an examination. The assumptions about education here are that it is to do with the transmission of knowledge; that knowledge is whatever can be propositionally stated; and that the teacher's function is to impart such knowledge. Here we have, of course, a good old English tradition of education revered throughout the empire! Contrasted as the American and English perspectives appear to be, there are nevertheless similarities between the two. Neither of the teachers, for example, is interested in process. Both of them can claim considerable authority for the selection of what should be taught; and both of them can claim to measure the effectiveness of their teaching by testing what the pupil can reproduce, either in skill modification or in factual knowledge. Surely such examples must give curriculum planners an unambiguous sense of purpose and direction.

Their job would certainly be made easier if these two examples were representative of the drama scene. Speaking of the UK, it is true that a comparatively small number of children might be studying the history of theatre (and, regrettably, a much larger number of children study Shakespearian texts as if they too were propositional knowledge) but as far as performance is concerned, such training, although popular in schools since the sixteenth century, has usually been extra-curricular with little attention to training as such. Curiously, however, one aspect of performance training, that associated with 'elocution', as it used to be called, has hovered on the edge of our school system during this century. Although receding in importance during the past twenty years, nevertheless it still has 'colonial' pockets of influence, particularly among, for example, the 'English' whites of South Africa and, perhaps surprisingly, among a not insignificant number of teacher-trainers in Australia. I mention this as an example of an isolated activity persisting in the face of opposing philosophical currents, typifying the contradictions within the confused picture of drama education which the 1980s have inherited.

Two metaphors have been used to capture the examples I have given so far. The American example of training in performance skills, representing as it does the behaviourist trend in education, can be seen as the 'blank-slate' view of education with the teacher as the writer on the slate. The British transmission of knowledge view has been described as the 'empty pitcher' model; the teacher of course doing the filling with information. The latter metaphor, however, can only be applied to the most rigid and unimaginative examination devotees. Different metaphors have to be sought for the majority of drama teachers. In the UK a 'new' movement in drama teaching began just before the turn of the century with the classroom practice of a lively village school teacher, Mrs Harriet Findlay-Johnson, whose 'dramatic method' of making school subjects more exciting was admired and publicized by a board inspector, Mr E. Holmes (1911), who in his book, *What Is and What Might Be*, wrote:

In Utopia acting is a vital part of school life of every class, and every subject that admits of dramatic treatment is systematically dramatized. [Holmes 1911, p. 174]

Mrs Findlay-Johnson was persuaded to publish her own credo in *The Dramatic Method of Teaching* at about the same time. From the private sector of the educational system another charismatic teacher in the Perse School was recommending the 'play way' of education. This was Caldwell Cook (1917), who as an English teacher, found a dramatic approach to help his pupils enjoy great literature. These two innovators who were so obviously interested in the *process* of learning were part of a trend that was fundamentally to challenge assumptions about the nature of education. The new metaphor, taken from the evolutionist's view of biological maturation was introduced by a German, F. Froebel, who saw a school as a 'kindergarten' and its pupils as 'flowering seeds' with all the potential for growth, given the right environment. Froebel was extending into education the Rousseau-esque view of the child as good, with natural instincts which should be freely followed.

This view of education as a matter of helping pupils in their natural growth has had an enormous influence on the teaching of drama for it appears to reduce the teacher's status to that of 'gardener', patiently attending development, and it also reduces the subject status as it is maturation, not content, that really counts. There are, however, different ways of interpreting the seed metaphor, an indication of which appears even in these early pioneers of drama. Contrast the two following quotations, from Holmes and Cook, respectively:

The teacher must therefore content himself with the child's expansive instincts, fair play and free play. [Holmes 1911, p. 163]

The question of how to persuade a boy to feel responsibility for his own learning, and to realize that nothing can be taught him which he does not cause himself to learn, is perhaps the most difficult problem which a teacher has to face. [Cook 1917, p. 73]

Whereas Holmes seems to advocate freedom of personal expression, Cook is emphasizing the importance of responsibility for learning. Thus we have here in a nutshell the divergent views of the romantic school of such people as Montessori, A. S. Neill and, in drama, Peter Slade and to a lesser extent Brian Way; and of the progressive school of people like John Dewey and Jean Piaget and, in drama, Winifred Ward in America and Dorothy Heathcote in England, the former concerned to create a proper environment for natural growth, the latter stimulating engagement with the environment; the former emphasizing freeplay; the latter stressing insight and problem-solving.

The flowering-seed metaphor might seem as light-weight as the seed itself. And yet the history of drama in education during this century is a record of various pioneers attempting to adopt this romantic progressive view. The need to 'hold childhood in reverence' (Rousseau), has dominated their philosophy if not their practice. Indeed apparent incompatibility of philosophy and practice seems to be a not uncommon feature of our pioneers. The romantic in Cook caused him to entitle his book *The Play Way* (1917), but his pupils finished up as expert performers of Shakespeare; the romantic in Peter Slade (1954) based his philosophy on child play (a markedly different concept from Caldwell Cook's 'playway'), yet he recommended the circumscribed practice of children re-enacting a story; the romantic in Brian Way (1967) respected the 'individuality of the individual' and yet his book is full of Stanislavskian-type exercises for the teacher to impose on all his pupils at the same time; the romantic in Dorothy Heathcote respectfully believes that children can know more than she does and yet she does not hesitate to assess with devastating accuracy what their learning needs might be.

That there is this ambiguity, that our drama pioneers have often failed to iron out apparent contradictions, should as we shall see, not be interpreted as a weakness but as a strength, (even though it causes distressing headaches in the meantime!) for the promotion of a uni-focused ideal in education in general seems to turn back on itself with no ready alternative within it that could be harnessed quite naturally for change. In America, for example, teachers are faced with accepting behaviourism or rejecting it with little room for ambiguity, or if one takes an example of another American movement which, as John Deverall (1979) has pointed out, has critically affected education in Australia while skirting the UK: the trend of humanism, one can detect that teachers have either rejected it out of hand or have taken on board a distorted version. It is sad to read Abraham Maslow (1974) in possibly his last published essay writing as follows:

30

The growing insistence of students that they be stimulated, inspired, entertained by the teacher may be taken as a symptom of the extreme child-centering of recent decades. [Maslow 1974, p. 63]

There has, incidentally, been a drama misinterpretation of the humanist movement which, at its most extreme has led to a self-indulgent spontaneity which eschews the disciplined hard work that Maslow and Carl Rogers (1961) before him intended. When I visited Australia in 1978 the fear expressed by drama teachers that what I was going to offer was 'psychodrama' was but an understandable reaction to the over-introspective 'sensitivity' drama of the 1970s.

This need to reject a philosophy has led to 'positions' and 'camps' and 'labels' (I was recently accused of failing to use the 'Gavin Bolton' method!). It is for this reason I think the standpoint of drama teachers in the 1980s is a healthier one: we are no longer so critical of apparent contradictions in the work of our pioneers; we seem more able to contain a dialectic of opposites in our philosophy; we are more inclined to see drama as multi-faceted; we can now, chameleon-like, adapt our subject to changing circumstances without denying its real nature. The rest of education may at this moment in time be rushing lemming-like 'back to basics'. Conceptually, for drama teachers this is no problem (although economically and politically their subject is, at least temporarily, threatened) for drama *is* basic, as I hope to demonstrate in the following discussion. Furthermore, whereas the dichotomy between traditional, subject-centred education and romantic/progressive child-centred education (or as it is being referred to in some quarters, between liberal and radical education) continues, drama manages to rise above this through its dialecticism.

I now propose to examine the truth of these claims in terms of the perspective I gave at the beginning: assumptions about education and knowledge; assumptions about the status of the subject; and assumptions about the status of the teacher.

Assumptions about education and knowledge

Richard Pring (1976) succinctly describes the dilemma of education. He claims, quite rightly, I think, that education is to do with the development of the individual's mind. He goes on:

Central to the development of mind is the growth of knowledge, and central to this is the refinement and extension of the conceptual framework through

31

which experience is organised. There is a difficulty however which needs to be resolved. The learner is an individual with a particular way of organising *his* experience, whilst the conceptual structures we seek to introduce him to are of others' making.   [Pring 1976, p. 23]

This dichotomy between 'knowing' as the organization of personal experience and 'knowledge' as something independent of the knower, divides educationists into opposing factions which can be represented by the following quotations:

The traditional/liberal view
This is what makes 'initiation' an appropriate word to characterise an educational situation; for a learner is 'initiated' by another into something which he has to master, know or remember.   [Peters 1967, p. 3]

What is clear, however, is that, if our training methods are not to remain the hit and miss business they are at the moment, the careful detailed analysis of the logical features of exactly what we wish to teach must be pursued.   [Hirst 1967, p. 60]

The progressive/radical view
In teaching a child we are trying to help the child make sense of things for himself.   [Curtis 1978, p. xx]

. . . in the gaining of knowledge, process and content are inextricable to the extent that process actually becomes an inherent part of the content.   [Harris 1979, p. 177]

A principal difference between these two sets of quotations lies in their assumptions about reality. The first two place an emphasis on public knowledge of the objective world that has to be passed on to the next generation, the second two give credence to the learner's view of the objective world. The peculiar position of drama is that it can successfully contain both these in a perpetual balance. The activity of drama requires from the participant an 'as if' mental set. This particular representational act, while sometimes appearing to be an escape from reality (the very word 'make-believe' or 'pretence' conjures up something that is not true) in fact, by definition, must have something external to the participant as a point of reference. His actions will either bear a verisimilitude to the objective world in so far as he understands it or will be a deliberate distortion with no less a grasp on what is being distorted. If a child in symbolic play successfully repeats some typical actions of his mother, he is patently involved in imitation of the objective world. If he deliberately exaggerates his real perception of those typical actions they nevertheless still provide the base-line for his egocentric behaviour. Even where there appears to be no imitation of anything recognizable as his mother's overt behaviour, there will inevitably be a conscious adoption of something to do with his mother – perhaps her attitude or her situation. There will be some aspect, therefore, even where there is distortion that could be judged by an observer to be true or false.

The same applies to drama. However uniquely personal a child's investment in what he is creating may be there will always remain some criterion of appropriateness in terms of something other than itself. This is not to say that all drama, like a simulation game, corresponds as closely as possible with the environment for this would, in Richard Pring's words, reduce art to 'a slightly bizarre way of giving an empirical account of the world' (Pring 1976, p. 44). What I am saying is that a degree of objectivity is necessary to any kind of dramatic activity. Necessary but not sufficient, that is. For the significance of drama lies in its concern with a process of *personal engagement* with the objective world, not in merely mirroring it. In other words, as in the Kevin Harris quotation above, process does become an 'inherent part of the content'. Drama is simultaneously subjective and objective.

What is learnt as drama may only partially (and least importantly) be spelled out in propositional terms. 'American Indians conduct a "pow-wow" ' may be a fact a child is able to articulate after his drama. But the experience may have resonated all kinds of 'intuitive', 'sensed' meanings not reducible to propositions. We are sometimes ready to rush to discuss our drama experiences in approximate 'knowledge that' forms, failing to recognize that the central experience of drama is what Arnaud Reid (1980) calls 'knowing this'.

This implied relationship between the knower and the known will be further elaborated in the next section.

Assumptions about the status of the subject

a   Drama as knowledge

Although Arnaud Reid refers to the occurrent knowing of art as 'knowing this', when he uses the expression 'knowing that' he is referring to knowledge *about* art, not as I shall continue to use it here in connection with that aspect of the art content that has an objective reference. We have to distinguish, therefore, among *three* kinds of knowledge in connection with drama: knowing about the subject, which is what O- and A-level candidates would be familiar with, knowing how to do drama, which falls within our earlier tradition of training in stage-crafts, and knowing or understanding the substance of a particular drama. It is in the latter sense that teachers are justified in pointing out that drama is a kind of parasite, not having a subject-matter of its own.

But it is this particular usage that distinguishes current trends in drama teaching from earlier movements. I detect two principal sources for this particular emphasis: in the work of Dorothy Heath-cote and in the practice of Theatre-in-Education teams. Both are concerned with using drama to teach something worthwhile, and that 'something' could come from anywhere in the curriculum. There has been a fair amount of resistance to these kinds of aims from practising teachers and even the Schools Council (1977) shied away from study-ing this emphasis in any depth, preferring to take refuge in the notion of drama for social skills or drama as dramatic statement. One of the problems for teachers is that it requires a skill in structuring at a more refined level of precision than previous trends have required. But there are other more fundamental reasons for teacher resistance which I hope to make clear as we look more closely at what is meant by teaching and learning in this context.

As already noted, at a superficial level drama can be concerned with the teaching and learning of facts. For example, Dorothy Heathcote recently taught a class of 9- to 10-year-olds about a shoe factory, using the children in role as employees. They learnt a great many facts about leather and shoe-making processes. Much more important however was that the kind of personal engagement, referred to above, brought about an attitude in the children of respect for craftsmanship and the responsibility of craftsmanship. At another level, however (and this brings us to the crux of the matter), Dorothy was planning for cognitive development. She wanted these children over the few ses-sions of drama to learn about 'change', the need for change, what brings about change and the effects of change. Before we look at the implications here, let me use another example – from my own teach-ing this time. A few weeks ago I was working with a class of top juniors on the problems of 'safety precautions' in a zoo where wild animals have to be secured from the public and yet available for the public to enjoy. The children were in-role as architects, involved in elaborate designs of cages and compounds, detecting flaws in each others designs and verbally sharing their findings. In the second lesson they were required in small groups to demonstrate by enactment how the most perfect safety precaution was not perfect enough. It was during the preparation of their demonstration that they stumbled on the significance of 'human error', a revelation that allowed the final discussions to take on a sobering aspect: to what extent can the safety of nuclear reactors be guaranteed as long as we have to rely on the human factor?

If we look at these two illustrations in terms of cognitive development the central concepts may be summarized as 'implications of change' and 'implications of safety'. No one could deny these are concepts of some consequence and of relevance to children of all ages. And yet given the educational 'establishment' view of the curriculum, these concepts would not normally be taught. By the 'establishment' view, of course, I am referring to Paul Hirst's reductionist's classification of the curriculum into seven subject 'disciplines'. Hirst is not only preoccupied with propositional knowledge but is determined to limit what is taught to the concepts that are fundamental to each major discipline. It is my opinion that such is the stranglehold that the reductionist/propositional theory has on our British school system that it is virtually impossible for some teachers to break out of it. They find it very difficult to identify the central concepts in a drama experience because all their thinking as pupils, students in teacher-training and as teachers, has been circumscribed by the notion of *subjects*, so that concepts have to be 'subject' concepts. 'Change' and 'safety' may be concepts that are critical to our common experience but they are not amenable to the categorical labelling of Hirst and other curriculum planners such as DES (1981) and the Schools Council (1981).

It seems that the concepts we deal with in drama are more fundamental to living than subject classification will allow. It is in this sense that the popular claim that drama is about life can be justified, for there is a distinct danger that when Hirst and his disciples reduce the objective world to logical, propositional forms, what really needs to be learnt by our pupils gets left out.

Curiously, I have only come across one non-drama publication in which the authors (Postman and Weingartner, 1971) in suggesting the kinds of concepts they consider could most usefully be learnt in school as part of an alternative, radical education, come very close to 'drama' concepts. Indeed, in reading their list I recognize some of the themes I have actually seen groups tackling in their drama work. I give a selection from their long list below:

How do you want to be similar to or different from adults you know when you become an adult?

How can you tell 'good guys' from 'bad guys'?

How can 'good' be distinguished from evil?

Where do symbols come from?

Where does knowledge come from?

What do you think are some of man's most important ideas?

How do you know when a good idea becomes a bad idea or a dead idea?

What is progress?

What is change?

What are the most obvious causes of change? What are the least apparent?

What's worth knowing? How do you decide?

These kind of questions cut across or go beyond subject divisions and yet they are basic to living. They seem to be ignored or dismissed by educationists.

Even Mary Warnock (1977) whose balanced view of curriculum theory I often appreciate, while going so far as to acknowledge the radical challenge of Postman and Weingartner, seems to be dismissive without good reason of what they are trying to say. She writes:

It is worthy of note, in passing, that the enquiry lessons quoted with approval by these authors almost all turn out to be on questions such as 'what counts as a rule?' Is there one and only one sense of 'right' and 'wrong'? 'Can there be different versions of the truth?', and so on.   [Warnock 1977, p. 67]

But although one might reasonably share her view that a whole curriculum made up of these kinds of enquiries would be ridiculous, one might nevertheless have expected that she would give them the serious consideration they deserve. She goes on:

All these questions are, roughly speaking, philosophical. And there is no doubt at all that children of all ages, as well as grown ups, enjoy talking about them. But even the most extreme proponent of the co-operative or enquiry method of education, or the most self-interested professional philosopher, would hardly suggest that this is to be the whole of the curriculum. And even when philosophy is to be the subject, a teacher will probably be a better philosopher than his pupils and will certainly have more expertise. [Warnock 1977, p. 67]

In my view it is these very 'philosophical questions' that children come face to face with in their drama. Part of the subject's status lies in its potential for putting children in touch with the very basic values of life.

To put the whole discussion so far on the status of the subject in summary form: it seems that when we emphasize the particular content of drama as critical for education we imply two conceptual levels of learning – the factual level relating to knowledge of the objective world and another more significant philosophical level often relating to one's responsibility towards the objective world (including oneself as part of that world). But this is only one side of the 'drama' coin.

b Drama as aesthetic form

The reader may have detected that in the two lesson illustrations I chose, we had instances of good education but weak drama. It could be argued that if the former is guaranteed who cares about the latter? Well curriculum planners do! From the discussion so far it would appear they would have very little to plan. For it is quite clear that Dorothy and I were *using* drama as any primary school teachers, non-drama secondary subject-specialists and remedial secondary teachers could. All it requires is for any teacher to put his pupils in the 'as if' mental-set so that they can engage with any kind of subject-matter in this special way.

Merely to use the psychology of dramatic action in this functional way (valuable as it might be) is in my view to fall short of the art experience which I consider should be part of a child's total education. First we have to examine what I mean by 'art experience' in drama. Historically two contrasted claims have been made by teachers for drama as art – by those who trained children in the art of performance and by disciples of Peter Slade who claimed that child drama is 'an art form in its own right'.

Now although I have taken up considerable space in arguing for the importance of subject-matter, i.e. what a particular drama is about, it seems to me that a drama teacher must simultaneously be teaching the 'how' of drama and that there will inevitably be times when the 'how' will be more important than the content, whether this be at the simplest level tackled by Dorothy Heathcote in her 'shoe-factory' lesson where she had to spend a fair slice of time giving the children confidence to make the imaginative leap into making shoes that were not really there or at a more sophisticated level of introducing stage design to a CSE examination class. But I want to go further than this. Whereas I do not agree with Peter Slade that child drama has its own art form, it seems to me that children must be trained to become aesthetically aware, i.e. *conscious of dramatic form*. They are not likely to achieve this if their drama experience is confined to 'mantle of the expert' kind of role-play at its purely functional level described in the two illustrations. They must, over their school years, acquire the basic drama/theatre skills of selecting focus, injecting tension and creating meaningful symbols (I have written about this at length elsewhere, Bolton, 1979). Given that these *basic* skills are acquired, the old drama–theatre dichotomy becomes redundant, not of course if the emphasis is still placed on the naturalistic Stanislavskian type of performance so long cherished by traditionalists who place the emphasis on performance techniques rather than on a fundamental understanding of the art form.

Notice I use the word 'acquired' rather than 'taught'. 'Consciousness of dramatic form' is something often sensed at a tacit level of comprehension. Although, as already remarked upon, neither of these illustrations was aesthetically strong, briefly, within each of them a move in the direction of drama as art took place – in two quite contrasted ways. At a critical point in Dorothy's series of lessons there suddenly occurred a confrontation between the employees of the factory and a stranger (teacher in role) who was actually seated at the boss's desk impatiently waiting for them to clock on at work. Here were all the elements of theatre; surprise, tension and teacher's selection of role as a 'time and motion' official, symbolizing through officialdom and territory take-over the very theme of the whole series – facing 'change'. This was a classic example of a change of dramatic level achieved by the 'spectator' role in the children responding to the teacher's theatricality. In other words, the children were not *themselves* actively engaged in creating an art form – but the teacher was! This important 'half-way house' gives the children an aesthetic experience at a subconscious level before they are ready to carry the responsibility.

By contrast, in my lesson, the children were required to be theatrical in a way that young children can safely handle. Because it is protected by the *task*, to use Goffman's (1974) term, it gives 'permission to stare'. They were in the crudest form of performance mode when they, in small groups, enacted how the most perfect safety precautions could go wrong: they were 'demonstrating' their solution – rather like a TV chef demonstrating baking a cake. Again they could be said to be 'acquiring' the skills of theatre for they were selecting for clarity of communication – not consciously to create theatre but to meet the requirements of the task.

It seems to me that a secondary specialist may sometimes be working in an art form with the participants (in a non-performance mode), only tacitly responding to its dynamic; at other times he may be encouraging them consciously to work for tension and symbolization etc. Similarly, he may make decisions in respect of performance – of the degree to which the pupils should concentrate on form.

Assumptions about the status of the teacher

The concept of authority and the teacher has been given a great deal of attention by educationists in recent years. Whereas it has always been seen as a critical factor varying between the two extremes of the teacher-dominated traditional and behaviourist's classrooms to the pupil-centred romantic/progressive/humanist's 'healthy environment' classrooms, a recent interest in the nature of knowledge and the education process taken by sociologists of education, such as Michael Young (1971) and Geoffrey Esland (1971), has led to a radical challenge of a teacher's authority. The new claim is that not only do most teachers improperly take it upon themselves to decide which public knowledge is important and how it should be taught, but they further use their power to control what is to count as knowledge. What should happen, according to these writers, is that the teacher should reduce his own authority by respecting that a pupil's perspective on knowledge is just as legitimate as his teacher's, for knowledge is socially constructed and whether it is true or false depends where you happen to be standing at the time.

As one would expect, big guns have been turned on this kind of argument; on this 'relativist' view. In untypically militant tones Mary Warnock writes, 'For if creeping relativism is not rooted out, then it seems to me that educationalists might as well shut up shop.' (Warnock 1977, pp. 107–8). The implication of relativism for Mary Warnock is that if 'anything goes' then you cannot plan a curriculum. Which brings us close to the dilemma of the drama teacher who in recent years has often found himself asking his classes, 'What do you want to make a play about?' What could be more 'relative' than this? Few other subject-teachers invite their classes to make choices of this order, so does this put drama teachers in a radical camp where pupils are leading their teacher? Not entirely, for the invitation to choose is often not as open as it sounds, for the teacher knows there are really going to be what Geoff Gillham (1974) describes as two plays: the play for the children *and* the play for the teacher. A clever teacher will blend these two so that the final drama experience meets both the pupils wants *and* the teacher's intentions. Teacher-status is then ambiguous. Although in my view such teacher manipulation is often justified (Dorothy Heathcote has coined the term 'benign manipulator') we must not be surprised if our critics charge us with dishonesty.

A further example of ambiguity (or dishonesty – depending on where you are standing) is often revealed in a drama teacher's attempt at being 'the one who doesn't know'. Mary Warnock strikes home when she compares the traditional teacher with the enquiry (child-centred) teacher: 'The difference between this and "ordinary" teaching becomes very obscure: the only addition seems to be that the enquiry teacher, like a skilful negotiator, has to pretend that the other party had the idea himself.' (Warnock 1977, p. 66). It is interesting to compare Mary Warnock's and Kevin Harris's attitude to the model of Socrates as a good non-authoritarian teacher. In the Meno he is seen leading a slave to display his knowledge of geometry. Harris respectfully quotes the well-known passage seeing it as an epitome of 'dialogical encounters, wherein teachers and learners together came to discover the real relationships that exist in the world they are exploring. . . .' (Harris 1979, p. 175) Mary Warnock refers to the same passage in these terms: 'For nothing could possibly be more artificial, not to say bogus, than the famous passage in the Meno. . . .' (Warnock 1977, p. 66) Artificial or not the 'Socratic method' is the approach which many drama teachers have adopted.

There is something about drama and the use of teacher-in-role in particular that does indeed make the teacher–pupil relationship more flexible. Teachers who perhaps in teaching, say, English would take a more traditional authoritarian stance, in switching to drama seem to relax their grip to a point where they might agree with Kevin Harris that their responsibility lies '. . . in helping others in the *common pursuit* of knowledge' (Harris 1979, p. 181). Dorothy Heathcote sees this loosening of the teacher's grip as a process of handing over power to the children. Again sceptics might perceive this as more apparent than real: they may feel that, paradoxically, in practice the greater the autonomy invested in the pupils, the greater is the power of influence retained by the teacher. Harris is condemning the traditional situation when he writes as follows:

A person can learn x (that less dense liquids float on more dense liquids). He can also learn x in a power situation, where someone determines that he shall learn it and someone makes him learn it – even if in the most pleasant ways. In both situations he comes to know x; but in the second situation he comes to know y (that someone determined that he learn x, and that someone made him learn x). Now x and y, in this situation or any similar situation cannot be totally disentangled, and so gaining knowledge of x is to some extent distorted, since *part of the experiential situation of coming to know X is knowing Y as well*. [My italics] [Harris 1979, p. 179]

But supposing a benevolent drama teacher subtly sets up a situation which allows the pupil to reconsider some concept of significance to the pupil's life (let us, too, call it x) will not his learning of x be just as influenced by the teacher's structuring (y) as by the most traditional teaching? Indeed is there not a chance that the teacher's influence will be the greater because his teaching was covert? If this is the case the status of the drama teacher is more powerful than it has ever been, even when he was allowed to be the most dictatorial director of the school play.

Summary

In this chapter I have attempted to show that the contribution of drama to education depends on what general educatonal philosophy is in the air, or what status is given to drama as knowledge and on the degree and kind of authority a teacher can exploit.

41

Tracing the historical development of drama in education it becomes clear that only in extreme instances could a coherent combination of these three factors be found: most often there has been confusion or even incompatibility. This, I maintained, should be seen as a strength, for contradictions provide the means for growth and change. Indeed in examining the above three perspectives in terms of current practice a number of dichotomies have emerged.

In looking at present-day assumptions about education and knowledge, the opposing philosophical positions of having respect for either a body of knowledge or for the knower appears to be contained by drama for, as we have seen, it can be both subjective and objective (a view not held, incidentally, by the education and the arts philosophy of Robert Witkin [1974] and Malcolm Ross [1978] who still follow 'an arts as personal expression' line).

The status of the subject itself is critically different from any previous trend. It is no longer (as a matter of priority) concerned with techniques or free expression or learning about theatre but is seen as a vehicle for cognitive development giving significance to the learning of those kinds of concepts which, while cutting across the traditional subject barriers, are nevertheless of central importance to living.

Concurrent with this usage of drama should occur the teaching (often indirect) of dramatic form – at a level more fundamental than acting techniques, a level that dissolves the rigid distinctions drawn in the past between drama and theatre by harnessing what they have in common.

But perhaps the greatest change is manifested in the status of the teacher who appears to be poised between opposing forces: he seems to offer choice with one hand while taking it away with the other; he seems to respect the perspective his pupils have of the world while tightly structuring for change; he seems to build up his own authority while giving power to his pupils. Somehow or other good drama teachers do find a logic within all these contradictions. It seems to me that the art of teaching requires this degree of flexibility and I would go so far as to say that in this respect teachers of drama may be ahead of their colleagues.

What hope to curriculum planners have of locating drama's position at an intersection of the three perspectives when the strands between them pull in so many different directions? I think there can be only one answer. They must plan for diversity and let the teachers in schools operate just as flexibly or inflexibly, broadly or narrowly and ambitiously or modestly as their personal security allows.

42

2 Drama and curriculum models

Terry Jones

I am always fascinated by gardening books. Lavish illustrations show luxurious shrubberies, abundant fruit, large pools covered with opulent lilies, the surface rippling with water cascading over rock and slate. For some people, such attractions are a stimulus: a challenge to create similar landscapes within their own acres. For most of us it is merely a dreamscape; a sight of how things might be if only we had the space. All things would then be possible.

Or would they?

Given the space, would I really have the time, the energy, the commitment and the skill to create a natural paradise; or would I show visitors my barren land and explain that I was far too busy, that the soil was of poor quality, that my neighbours had a better water supply . . . ?

Green-fingered drama teachers will be quick to point out that an environment can be transformed by a window-box or a few pot-plants; that intention counts for more than resources.

To continue the analogy for a moment longer: I frequently gaze in admiration at the allotment next to mine. As I struggle with couch grass, nettle and mare's tail, the man on the next plot – without a weed in sight – inspects and collects his produce. Bathed in sweat, I ask him how he does it. 'Don't worry,' he says, 'it'll come right – just time and feeding – time and feeding!' none of which allays my frustration.

I hear similar frustrations expressed by drama teachers in their schools and on courses. After lectures or during discussions, it is not unusual to hear 'It's all very well suggesting x or y . . . but if you were in my situation . . . !' How realistic are such comments? How much do the arrangements made for drama in particular schools affect the nature of the drama teaching itself?

The function of this chapter is to examine the way in which drama is (or can be) organized in schools. There are other resource factors, such as space, equipment and finance, which teachers will claim have a major affect on what kind of drama work they can undertake. These things are important but the organization of drama within the curriculum as a whole is the base from which all other concerns spring.

There is increasing debate on what should go into the secondary curriculum and – by implication – what may safely be left out! It may well be that there are schools who display the same curriculum – the educational diet offered to the children – that has existed in that school for twenty years or more. Fortunately, such schools are becoming more difficult to find. Schools are finding it (rightly) impossible to avoid the pressures that come from a variety of agencies outside the institution itself. Depending on individual perceptions, these pressures may be welcomed or greeted with suspicion. Eventually, however, the result of these pressures is that change takes place and the curriculum is adjusted and a new shopping-list of subjects appears. If all children are to be offered more health education, political education, computer education, personal, social and moral education . . . and if the arts in general and drama in particular are to be protected, then perhaps we should strive to change the focus of the current debate. Discussions which centre on 'Shall we cut A in order to include B' threaten the morale of teachers as well as activities which are educationally worthwhile. It may be far more constructive to discuss the patterns of learning within the school: the way subjects are organized and the time that is needed for different activities.

Many teachers might wish to question the whole notion of a subject-centred curriculum. Such thoughts are hardly original but given the present organization of our secondary schools it would be philosophical speculation to deal with them here, and drama teachers might find such issues too far from their own reality to have any significance as yet.

Whether there is an ideal way of organizing drama in schools is open to debate. I shall describe three schools in which differing arrangements are made for drama and then reflect on those differences.

Essentially, I have chosen these actual (but anonymous) schools because the quality of drama teaching is (in my opinion) high.

It would, of course, be possible to find other examples to suit every prejudice of every reader: poor quality work because drama is organized in this way; excellent work because drama is organized in that way.

My thesis will be that different methods of organizing drama do not, of themselves, affect the quality of the work done. Only the philosophy, understanding and skill of the teacher will affect that – together with his or her relationship with the children or students. I will go on to argue that however positive these elements may be, teachers may be either consciously or unconsciously hampered by the form of curriculum organization within which they work.

School A

Drama as the responsibility of the English department

This is a rural, 11–16 school with 600 pupils. It is organized as a 4 FE school with a separate remedial group in the first year.

First year
Second year } Each form has a single 50-minute period of drama per week
Third year

Fourth year } One option group in each year following a drama examination course – 3 × 50-minute periods
Fifth year

Drama teaching and its development in the school is the direct responsibility of the head of English, Mr Smith. Half of his own timetable is drama, an indication of his very strong interest in the subject. He succeeded another head of English with an equally strong conviction about the value of drama. There is no doubt that drama is seen as being a normal, well-established part of the curriculum. That is not to imply, however, that this is necessarily an ideal way of organizing drama. This is a point I shall develop below.

Whether the mechanics of the organization affects the work that is done must be a major question throughout this chapter. In this school I suspected that group work in English would inevitably carry over into drama sessions. However, another piece of organization seems to prevent this. Classes are taught in sets for English but come to drama in mixed-ability tutor groups. There is some overlap but Mr Smith cannot assume that a drama class will have had a common experience in English.

Clearly, Mr Smith sees his role in the school as combining head of

45

English and drama specialist. A committed and sensitive teacher, he aims to give the pupils a wide range of drama experiences and is particularly skilled at teacher role-play. The only time when an 'English' approach to drama is discernible is during that part of the summer term when the hall is used for examinations. At that time, themes are explored through drama in a classroom and developed in writing. I must stress that this is a minor part of the drama programme and that the majority of the work appears unaffected in content and style by its ties with an English department.

There are other ways in which those ties can be seen to have an effect. Mr Smith not only teaches drama: he protects it. Although he feels that drama should 'ideally be autonomous', it is likely (in a school of this size) that a full timetable would not be found for a drama specialist, whereas Mr Smith – as a senior head of department – can negotiate with senior staff to ensure that time and resources are made available for drama.

I said earlier that I had no wish to imply that this was an ideal method of organizing drama within the curriculum. In this school it works: but it works because of the commitment of the teacher – a commitment which is to drama *per se* and not to drama as an adjunct to studies of dramatic literature, as is often the case. Of course drama can be used, valuably, to explore themes and ideas that children encounter in English studies but that is a very restrictive use of drama teaching. Caldwell Cook (1911) was clearly a highly innovative teacher of English when he came to the Perse School in Cambridge in 1911. When he introduced his 'Playway' methods it was in the belief that genuine learning and understanding would come through action. He was, however, mainly concerned with enlivening and enlightening the dull study of texts. Seventy years have shown that the use of drama is far more wide-reaching.

My final concern about organizing drama within English departments is not only that it can be restrictive but that it can be a recipe for inaction. Where schools claim that 'our English department looks after the drama', I have often found an extremely patchy programme. One or two English teachers will develop their drama work with enthusiasm; others in the same department will have little interest or confidence in drama teaching and their pupils will have no experience in this area of expressive learning. Others may relegate drama to the end of term, when other aspects of their syllabus have been covered, and a few superficial charades can be acted-out.

I know English departments where drama is a vital part of their work: my comments on Mr Smith in school A illustrate this. My argument is simply that as a curriculum model, it is not one that usually begins with a strong commitment to drama in education and then seeks various ways to develop the activity over five or six years of a pupil's secondary education.

School B

The separate drama department

This is a very large 11–18 comprehensive school, taking all the pupils in the town. The drama department has three full-time staff and half a timetable from another teacher. The head of department, Mr Brown, is a man of considerable energy who has, over five years, considerably enhanced the status and credibility of drama within the school. In such a large school, the organization of drama appears complex:

First year
{ 14 mixed-ability tutor groups
1 single 35-minute period per week

Second year
{ 14 mixed-ability tutor groups
1 double 70-minute period per week

Third year
{ Drama is an option against music
Pupils may choose either:
(*a*) A single drama period *and* a single music period
or
(*b*) A double drama period *or* a double music period
At the time of writing, this option had resulted in:
12 teaching groups with a double period of drama
4 teaching groups with a single period of drama

Fourth year
Fifth year
{ A two-year 'recreational option' course is offered against music, PE and art. There are 6 groups taking drama in the fourth year and 5 in the fifth year

Sixth form
{ A one-year O-level drama course is on offer. There is one teaching group (5 periods). A recreational drama option is also available

Apart from the sheer volume of drama being taught, the most striking aspect of the department is the sense of cohesion between the staff.

This is largely due to the energy of Mr Brown and the support of his headmaster. The teachers meet frequently and hold consistent aims for the department. Within the overall programme, the children probably have as wide a range of drama experiences as is possible within the constraints of the school's resources and timetable.

Size apart, the curriculum pattern is fairly standard and relates fairly closely to School A. The differences, though apparently minor, are worth highlighting:

1   The first-year groups receive only 35 minutes for their weekly drama period. Though far from unusual, the majority of drama teachers find this far too short a period to stimulate any worthwhile drama activity. Some teachers point out that, on a large site, the lesson time may only be 26–7 minutes long – by the time the pupils have arrived.

Why 35 minutes? This may well be the length of the standard teaching module used to build up the timetable and many teachers may find it suitable for their own subject. The drama teacher may have these short periods because he or she insists on a weekly drama lesson with all classes. If they really are of little value, it is pointless telling colleagues that senior staff don't understand the nature of drama! There is point in making alternative proposals, the simplest of which might be a double period every two weeks. Whatever the proposal, it is crucial that the drama teacher should understand the timetable and the way it is constructed. Not, apparently, the most exciting of concerns but essential if the timetabler is to take curriculum proposals seriously.

2   The second point to note is the mini-option system between drama and music in the third year. This is another device for providing additional drama time – for those who want it! The whole question of options raises issues as much concerned with educational philosophy as with curriculum organization. Although it is not the purpose of this chapter, it is interesting to reflect that drama teachers who voice concerns about child autonomy and freedom of choice will also insist that all pupils should have at least X minutes or periods of drama per week.

3   I find the fourth- and fifth-year pattern fascinating, simply because none of the drama teaching is tied to examination work, which is, increasingly, becoming the norm.

I don't seek to make judgements for or against examinations in drama or theatre studies, but many teachers running such courses do so, they claim, because it is the only way to establish drama beyond the third year. School B shows that it is possible to offer a range of non-examination options (not just for the academically less-able) which are well supported.

In School B, the cohesion in Mr Brown's department indicates the potential strength and weakness of the 'separate department'. He lays stress on the fact that there is considerable opportunity for liaison between the four members of staff teaching drama. Such liaison will not only be reflected in discussions on departmental aims, but also in discussions on content, style and methods across year groups. The considerable energy of this department, therefore, focuses inward on its own concerns and activities and Mr Brown admits that there is very little liaison or communication with other subject areas. In a school as large as this, there are strong administrative reasons for organizing teaching on a department basis and drama certainly welcomes this.

While the department itself creates a dynamic for drama teaching, there are also political/professional reasons why departmental status is welcomed and these will be discussed later.

School C

Drama within a faculty system

This is an 11–18 comprehensive school, one of two in a market town. The school serves the town as well as the surrounding villages. There are four major faculties in the school and drama is part of the creative arts faculty. The 'senior subject teacher' responsible for drama is Mrs Green. As assistants, she has two members of staff each working a ⅔ drama timetable and four other teachers working in drama from two to six hours per week. The pattern of drama teaching is as follows:

First year { 1 hour of drama per week
Second year { (similarly, 1 hour of art and music)

Third year *Fourth year* *Fifth year*	{ 1½ hours of creative arts per week

Note:

a In this context, 'creative arts' are taken to mean music, art and drama – although design technology, wood and metal work, home economics and dress also come within the faculty

b In the first term of the third year the three subjects are offered in three-week cycles

c For the remainder of the three years the subjects are organized, as nearly as possible, in half-term blocks.

Fourth year *Fifth year*	{ Drama examination courses are offered in three option blocks. There are three drama teaching groups in both the fourth and fifth years – each having 2½ hours per week

Sixth form   A-level drama course: 5 hours teaching in each year

Before looking at the notion of the faculty system in general, there are three points which emerge from the facts above:

a School sizes apart, there is a greater amount of drama activity here than in Schools A and B. This is a direct result of the quality of Mrs Green's teaching and her excellent relationships with pupils. This has made drama popular with the children and the headmaster has been prompt in his support of curriculum areas which are seen to be working well.

b It is also the philosophy of the headmaster that if an area of experience is important in the early years, then that area of education should be carried into the fourth and fifth years – irrespective of any option system connected with examination courses. School C is the only school of the three where every pupil will have some experience of drama through the first to the fifth year. In addition, we can see that there are six examination option groups in the fourth and fifth years – another indication of the popularity of drama.

c The organization of drama in the first term of the third year may, at first, seem at odds with the rest of the pattern. It is an attempt to come to terms with the option system and the 'circuit' system frequently associated with faculties. This system – elsewhere called a 'circus' or 'arts roundabout' – is simply a method of trying to include all subjects within a finite amount of available time.

The result is that, in these three years, a pupil will have drama for half a term, followed by similar periods of art and music. In School C, pupils make their initial option choices at the end of the autumn term of the third year. Staff were concerned that, if a pupil has not been given experiences of all arts subjects in that autumn term, they would have an unfair base on which to make an option choice. I am not sure whether this fear is justified but I can certainly understand a teacher's concern to maintain viable option groups in the fourth and fifth year.

I have encountered a few schools which have offered drama options in the fourth and fifth year without any drama teaching in the lower school! In two such schools, the options failed totally to recruit pupils after one or two years of initial enthusiasm.

There is no doubt that the whole range of problems associated with the 'circuit' organization has become widespread with the development of faculty systems in schools. So widespread, in fact, that it is worth looking at the faculty concept in general terms before concluding comments on School C.

The two arguments normally rehearsed for the faculty system were clearly stated by a headmaster when I asked him why he operated such a system.

I was becoming increasingly alarmed at my last school by the fractionalized timetable – especially in a large school. I thought I could see two virtues in faculties; one, the most important, the curricular reality – making a real study area; but the second one that I think is undervalued, but is very useful, particularly in a change situation, the administrative neatness. . . . The thing I think you've got to realize is that the curricular reality takes much longer. The temptation is that they will carry on with their old rationale in an administratively neat package.

The quotation neatly synthesizes the controversy surrounding the faculty debate. In a large school, timetabling becomes simpler if you can block large groups of children, say, half-year groups, with groups of teachers. That process becomes even simpler if there are readily indentifiable groups of teachers in the school and a faculty staff supplies that need. Opponents of the faculty system would say that this is the only advantage – an advantage to the timetabler above everyone else. An equally cynical argument might be that it is much easier to divide financial and other resources among a small group of faculty heads than cope with pressures from many individual members of staff. Those arguing for the system would point out that faculties combined with block timetabling create much greater flexibility: given a hundred-plus children, x periods of time and y teachers, the staff can decide on group sizes and the way in which they will divide their time among them.

It will also be argued that this flexibility relates not only to the organization of learning groups but also to decisions that are taken about teaching styles. Co-operative teaching is possible. Children can move (within the faculty) from teacher to teacher during a project, as educational needs dictate. That, at least, is the theory. The faculty would be a self-contained unit providing opportunities for the staff to take corporate decisions about curriculum content and teaching methods.

There is no doubt that some faculties have worked in this way but I believe them to be in a minority. A number of headteachers have told me that they do not believe the faculty system is a 'curricular reality' in their school and would gladly 'unravel the system' – if only they were able. That is not to imply that they do not have the authority or ability to institute such a change but, after a number of years, so many aspects of school life become intrinsically meshed into that system and effecting major change could be more destructive than leaving the faculty system as it is.

If faculties do provide the base for exciting educational collaboration and co-operation – and I believe they do – why have so many failed to work? I would briefly summarize the inhibiting factors as:

1 Which subjects go where? If faculties are to be more than an administrative contrivance, the subjects placed within those faculties must be clearly perceived by pupils and staff as having a relationship. They may share common skills or deal with similar areas of human understanding. Without that clearly perceived relationship, some faculty members may be forgiven for believing they have been 'lumped' together with other subjects for no apparent reasons.

2 Leadership. If the relationship between subjects is to develop into a reality for the children, the faculty head has a crucial role in welding together a team with different skills and encouraging a corporate policy. I have met many faculty heads who see themselves as administrators of the faculty and who, for various reasons, are content to let subject teachers within their faculty do their own thing.

3 Subject autonomy. If some faculty heads feel that it would be

professionally impertinent to 'interfere' with the work of specialist teachers, the reverse is also frequently true. There are many teachers who believe – and often state forcefully – that they were appointed to teach history, music, physics, or whatever, and that their work, in their subject with their pupils, is going to remain unaffected by the organization of the school. Further, they often feel that the status of their discipline is somehow tainted by any hint of collaboration or integration. Such attitudes are, sadly, understandable and spring both from the way we have, traditionally, organized knowledge in secondary education and from the way career development and promotions have come about.

4   Time. A faculty may provide opportunities, but it also imposes constraints and the allocation of time is one of the most obvious. If the 'quart into a pint pot' syndrome is a problem for education as a whole, it is seen clearly in creative or expressive arts faculties. It results in the 'circuit' organization referred to earlier and links with the subject autonomy argument. Teachers often feel that if their time with a particular group of pupils is to be limited – certainly less than they would wish – then they need that time 'for my subject'. In such an atmosphere, collaborative enterprises rarely flourish.

5   There are those who would argue that the very size and existence of the faculty inhibits curriculum development. In secondary schools organized on traditional lines, individual teachers have found it possible to make links with colleagues from other disciplines in order to mount specific projects. Such links (drama with history; literature with art) are often based on personal friendships and/or ideological consensus. When faculties appear, this kind of link often proves to be impossible. Traditional departments behind fences turn into faculties behind castle walls. The head I quoted above told me:

> The great danger is that a faculty begins to go into itself and begins to see itself as a fully autonomous unit within the school.

Returning to Mrs Green's work in School C, we can ask in what way the drama work is affected by the faculty organization. Apart from imposing the 'circus' organization, which Mrs Green dislikes, in the third, fourth and fifth years, there is virtually no other impact on drama work in the school. The faculty head is from the craft/design area and there is very little contact with the music, art and drama staff. The staff from these three subject areas do meet frequently, mainly to discuss the use of specialist and shared spaces. In the early days of the faculty, there were several attempts at integrated project work. Increasingly, however, staff have preferred to do their own thing, perhaps feeling that some of that early integration was somewhat artificial.

I know creative arts faculties that work extremely well, though they are in a minority. The hallmark of these is that they have tackled the factors (1–4) I listed above. Creating a faculty that is a 'curricular reality' is hard work and is certainly time-consuming. The ones I have in mind have spent endless hours of meetings discussing the different arts 'subjects', writing and re-writing policy papers, watching colleagues teaching and gradually evolving a sense of curriculum purpose.

The three ways of organizing drama within the school curriculum I have described are certainly the most common, though there will be inevitably differences from school to school. I have tried to emphasize the positive aspects of different methods of organization – recounting timetabling horror stories may make the reader wince or sympathize, but these would hardly be pointers to good curriculum practice.

There are other methods of organizing drama work and, though far less common, they raise interesting issues.

a Block release

Although I have no direct experience of this form of organization, it has proved successful in the schools where it has been operated. It is described in some detail in *Learning through Drama* (McGregor *et al.* 1977) and basically is an attempt to avoid the frustrations of a series of weekly, short periods (as in the first year in School B). So, for example, instead of a class having a single weekly 35- or 40-minute drama lesson over a term, the class is released for a whole day of drama, twice a term. Another example, quoted by the Schools Council team, was the teacher whose 'classes were receiving three and a half days of drama, two or three times per year'. Teachers who have worked with groups on weekend or residential courses will immediately recognize the advantages. The teacher and the group can, together, develop a rhythm of work which is appropriate to the nature of the drama being explored or constructed. Children are not summoned by bells just as the work is beginning to take off.

Though I would much prefer to work in this way, many teachers will feel that, however intense the experience may be, two or three encounters per year does not give them the sense of continuity they require.

b The floating teacher

I have met only one headmaster who positively encouraged this notion and, again, it had much to commend it. In effect, he appointed a drama specialist, who had no timetable. The teacher would make herself available to individual members of staff or departments and work with classes for a series of lessons. The theory was that the skills of the drama specialist would help the class explore themes, issues, concepts they were following in English, history, geography etc.

That experiment came to an end some years ago at the request of the drama teacher herself. It could be argued that the teacher felt that there were not enough demands on her services by other staff. I believe that today, with a greater use of role-play in education and a fuller understanding of enactive learning, such an experiment would stand a much greater chance of success. It is also probably true to say that the teacher rehearsed the 'continuity' arguments (in *a* above), feeling that weekly contact with pupils, via a traditional timetable, would enhance the development of drama in the school.

c Positive *laissez-faire*

I use the word 'positive' because I would not wish to confuse this approach to drama in the curriculum with that referred to at the beginning of the chapter, where heads hope that 'my English staff look after drama – as and when appropriate'.

In this case I am referring to specific headteachers I know who understand the value of drama in education and who would wish to see it permeate the curriculum of their school. However, they are reluctant to appoint a drama specialist, arguing that this would effectively stop other teachers attempting to use drama methods in their teaching. Their educational argument is a strong one. If drama can – as Gavin Bolton (1979) so vividly described in his own book – help children 'feel their way into knowledge', then surely this teaching style is too important to be left to one teacher who may eventually come, as one headteacher described, to 'occupy a cultural ghetto down the corridor'.

Whilst agreeing with their philosophy, I have to argue with the practical realism of the stance they take. Who is to give a large number of specialist teachers the drama skills they require – if, indeed, the individuals accept their head's philosophy? There is no sign that advisory or in-service opportunities are becoming more widely available – quite the reverse. Even if geographers, historians, RE teachers etc., became confident in the use of drama methods, who would develop drama and theatre studies with older pupils – if those studies are thought to be important?

Summary

I have referred to six ways in which drama can be made part of the curriculum. There will obviously be variations in detail but I see little value in distinguishing between 30-, 35-, 40-minute drama lessons. In discussions with drama teachers, I have found little consensus as to what constitutes an ideal curriculum model. Some teachers may feel that, in any case, these are hypothetical discussions: their timetable is fixed, is determined by the constraints of the school and cannot be changed.

Change is possible – particularly within a wider context of change and innovation. At the beginning of the chapter I referred to the way in which the secondary school curriculum was under considerable scrutiny for different reasons, which include:

a *Accountability* – Various sections of society (government, employers, parents) increasingly seek to influence what is taught in schools.

b *Falling rolls* – In many areas, student numbers are declining dramatically and, without major reorganization, it seems inevitable that many schools will decrease in size – and staff. As schools get smaller they will have to decide what constitutes a basic curriculum.

c *Pressure of 'new' subjects* – I have already listed some of the subjects claiming a place in what many think is an already over-crowded curriculum. Without resorting to such devices as a ten-day time-table, time available is finite and drama teachers, *inter alia*, must be prepared to rethink traditional teaching patterns.

The past decade was, in education, preoccupied with organization: how secondary education should, itself, be organized and how individual schools should best organize learning groups. That emphasis has swung to 'the curriculum' and is, I believe, likely to stay there for some years. In this situation, drama teachers should be taking a positive initiative – before it is taken for them.

In deciding what that initiative should be, there are three fundamental questions that must be faced:

1 What do the pupils need?
2 What does the school need?
3 What does the teacher want?

The problem lies in exploring the answers to questions 1 and 2 as honestly as possible and relating it to the answer to 3. It is too easy to assume that once question 3 has been answered, one has solved the problems inherent in 1 and 2. Drama teachers often reflect much of their own personal ideology in their professional behaviour – there is an extent to which avoiding this is impossible.

If, at the time of heightened curriculum awareness, the views of the drama teacher are to be listened to and respected, then it is important that his or her professional theory and practice are as coherent and consonant as possible. For example:

a If a drama teacher speaks longingly of the primary school ethos, where bells do not end lessons abruptly, and where children's interests and excitements can be explored when the time is right, does it then make sense for that teacher to argue for a weekly drama lesson with the first three years?
b If, at staff meetings, the drama teacher argues that 'given the opportunities, drama can have an all embracing relationship in the life of the school' (McGregor *et al*. 1977), can he also argue that that relationship will grow inside a separate drama department?
c If a teacher believes that drama is essentially a 'method' of teaching and learning, rather than a 'subject', is that belief made credible when that teacher insists on an examination group in theatre studies, merely in order to teach in the senior part of the school?

57

d   Conversely, many drama teachers came into the profession stimulated by their experience in school plays, youth and student theatre. With a major personal commitment to performance work, some teachers largely deny this in their schools, believing that the prevailing orthodoxy sees theatre as not 'the done thing'. If they believe that children's understanding can be enriched through a course of theatre skills, why not propose a performing arts course for those pupils who wish it?

e   If the drama teacher feels that the head, the timetabler and senior staff fail to understand his aims and objectives, have they lost the paper on which they were clearly laid out?

These questions are not intended to be contentious rhetoric. They are intended to provoke the simple notion that different drama teachers may have different objectives which may require different curriculum models.

I began teaching drama in 1958 and was, at that time, given a single period per week for the first, second and third years. I was perfectly happy to accept that position – after all, there were few heads as liberal as mine, one who would actually put drama on the timetable. Over twenty years later, the situation is very different. A great deal of thinking about the nature of drama in education has taken place and that thinking has been disseminated through writings, lectures, research projects, discussion and courses.

I cannot believe, after all that, that a single period per week is the best constructed curriculum model a drama teacher can offer or would want. That would be as banal as believing one could construct a year's drama work out of ninety-two games and five trust exercises.

I do believe that there are now many drama teachers who are working with time patterns that are totally inappropriate to their needs. I have already suggested that change is easier when change is 'in the air', than when the school is dedicated to the *status quo*. Change can be painful and the drama teacher who is seen to cause pain is less likely to achieve his or her objectives. Here, then, is a suggested check-list for action:

1   Sit down by yourself – or with your drama colleagues – and decide on the kind of drama you really wish to see happening in your school.

2   Put it on paper. Make it as descriptive as possible. Avoid jargon. Paint a picture.

58

3   Now look at that description. Discuss the patterns of time that you
believe would make it work for you.
4   What are the implications for the timetable? If the drama teachers
don't have a clear grasp of the mechanics of the timetable, bring a
friend in who does. Be he or she maths, science, or geography, they
don't need to understand your philosophy but can, very possibly,
give sound timetable advice.
5   When the timetable implications are clear . . . put them on paper.
Your careful preparation may not ensure a total acceptance, so
prepare a range of options: 'We need A – but B or C would be
infinitely preferable to D or E.'
6   If your implications are likely to affect other members of staff . . .
talk to them. Make certain that *all* those likely to be affected are
aware of your proposals. There have been occasions where staff-
room politics made Watergate look like *Playschool*: secret negotia-
tions usually cause resentment – avoid them.
7   Now that your proposals are clear, seek *formal* meetings with the
'change agents'. This may be a one-to-one meeting with the headteacher; a specially convened faculty head's meeting; a session of
the curriculum committee . . . whatever is appropriate to your
school.
8   Ensure that all meetings are clearly minuted and that papers are,
subsequently, circulated to everyone likely to be concerned.
9   Two final suggestions:
   a   This is a twelve-month process: attempting major change in two
   or three months is frequently a recipe for disaster.
   b   Avoid messianic zeal at all costs. Of course you care deeply – so
   do the teachers of home economics and environmental studies.
   Quiet clarity is far more likely to carry a staff meeting than impas-
   sioned speeches that suggest that colleagues don't understand the
   needs of drama.

To return to the garden.

I wish I had serried ranks of blight-free potatoes, immaculate cauliflowers and
sprouts.

I wish I could look out on a healthy pond I had created, fed by a waterfall,
surrounded by delicate alpines.

59

I wish my soil would grow asparagus – I'm sure I have the skill – something must be letting me down.

If I had more space, my soft fruits would be amazing.

With more heat, my orchids would win prizes.

If . . . if . . . if . . . if . . .

Perhaps I should stop dreaming – decide on my priorities – and stop blaming my soil.

'Time and feeding', said my neighbour.

3 The pastoral curriculum

Leslie Button

The whole school

It has been part of the tradition of British education that school is concerned with all round development, and this is a tradition that Britain has exported to a number of other countries. It is sometimes argued that a healthy daily routine is all that is required: that the spirit of the school will rub off on the pupils, and this is all the social training that is necessary. The argument often harks back to the small personal school, in which mutual knowledge and respect could form the basis for a healthy development of attitudes.

Times have changed, and there are grounds for the widespread anxiety about the relationships that exist in the larger school of today. It is not only a matter of size: there is a growing depersonalization in our society, and there has been a world-wide challenge to authority that has inevitably influenced attitudes and relationships in school. But it is still true that everything that goes on in school, every activity and every hour of the day carries with it a social and emotional message, which will have its impact on the experience and attitudes of all concerned.

The hidden curriculum

This is part of the hidden curriculum in school, and those who are planning pastoral programmes will need to bring to the surface and to make explicit these unseen influences. For example, how far does the school day make for personal responsibility on the part of young people for their behaviour and study, or does it merely demand conformity? And what is the long-term impact on the students' habits of study, and on their attitudes to life and to work? Similarly, is there a confusion between obedience and discipline? Is the term 'disciplining' used as a euphemism for 'punishing'? And is it appreciated that every time we give an order, especially about behaviour, we pre-empt the possibility of the young person concerned taking his own responsible action? I am not arguing that direction and firm leadership should not be exercised; I am only underlining the consequences that are all too frequently not acknowledged.

How far does the school regime grant personal significance to individual young people? The need for significance, to matter, is a basic human need, and we may find that young people will demand significance in opposition to the school if it is not granted by the school regime.

We could continue by putting into juxtaposition competition or collaboration with all that that implies, support or belittling, regimentation or individuality, and, especially involving the teachers, secretiveness and openness. The tradition of academic freedom has many advantages, but it can lead to an isolation and secretiveness that leaves some members of staff without the support that they need. As for methods of control, how much violence, in word as well as deed, takes place, and how much dialogue, compromise and collaboration? Teachers often complain of apathy in young people, but it is not always appreciated that apathy can be a valid adjustment to an irksome situation that the participants feel unable to influence.

Value positions

I am not wishing to argue that a regime should present one extreme or another: but it is important that what is taking place should be seen clearly and explicitly, because this is the point of departure for a pastoral posture. A value position is inescapable, and it is no less a value position if it remains unacknowledged. Perhaps it would be fair to the reader, at this stage, for me to acknowledge my own value position. I would hope that as a result of our pastoral work we will help young people to be self confident in their capacity to meet life as it comes, to be able to sustain responsible relationships, and play their part in an increasingly caring community. In these days of individual morality, young people are less likely to accept a given position and need to work out their own moral standards. Unless opportunities are given for this, there is a danger that young people will slip into an amoral style of life. We have the responsibility for challenging young people to feel their way towards a tenable position, but if we are serious about their personal responsibility in this, we may have to accept that they might challenge our position as we will challenge theirs.

So we may find ourselves turning a full circle: we will wish to question and make explicit the social and moral undercurrent of school life, which constitutes the hidden curriculum, at the same time accepting that there must inevitably be some kind of powerful influences embedded in the daily routine of the school. It is only that we would wish them to be as creative as possible. There is little point in conducting an explicit pastoral programme for the short time allotted to it, if much of the remaining experience in school pulls in another direction. It is urgent that the underlying social influences should be made accessible and visible, and for this we need a vocabulary and the necessary insights that will enable us to keep it under review.

It is not only in this sense that the pastoral programme is a whole school undertaking. A very large proportion of the staff in most schools are charged with the responsibility for the pastoral care of a group of between twenty-five and thirty young people. This means that pastoral policy touches the whole staff as nothing else in the school. This brings challenges that I will return to later in this chapter, but the fact that the pastoral programme involves the whole school also offers some very important opportunities.

The content

In looking at pastoral programmes and approaches, I shall be writing from a standpoint informed by an action research project, funded by the Leverhulme Trust Fund and the Health Education Council, which I have been conducting with the co-operation of panels of teachers in various parts of Britain, Ireland and several overseas countries. The resultant programmes are published under the title, *Group Tutoring for the Form Teacher* (Button 1981). These programmes, in turn, are built on earlier work – again an action research programme involving teachers, youth workers, and social workers – as a result of which models of work were established that I have called developmental group work (Button 1974).

Major themes

A number of main themes need to be sustained throughout the whole of a five-year pastoral programme. The themes will be picked up with differing intensity at certain times of each year.

The pupil's place in the school   Young people need to be engaged in a responsible contribution to and an active participation in the affairs of the school. It is important that pupils of all ages should feel involved, but the way in which it is expressed must respond to the age of the young people.

The pastoral group as a small, caring community   This is the basis upon which everything else is built. Support also involves challenges: support must not be confused with cosiness. The group needs to work out its own caring programme, and the tutor will need to help the young people to establish the style in which this is to be carried out.

Relationships, the self and social skills   Although this heading covers a very large area of concern, these elements are put together since they are so interdependent. The term 'relationships' is wide-ranging, including friendship, other peers, family, other adults, and people in authority. The development of social skills and self knowledge must be approached with increasing sophistication as the experience of the young people grows.

Communication skills   Very rapid progress can be made here. Being articulate includes being able to identify the internal concerns and issues that are waiting to be expressed. The skill of active listening and an interest in the other person underlies so much in life.

School work and study skills   Which are the areas of skill and concern that are common to all school work and can reasonably be dealt with within the pastoral programme? This section must especially be concerned with attitudes, anxieties and objectives, and with group support in moving towards these objectives.

Academic guidance in careers education   This is concerned with helping young people to know themselves and to move towards wise decisions. It would not be about ready-made advice: the initiative should be in the hands of the young people. The discussion of careers should be very much an educational programme about the world of work and other peoples' lives, and not narrowly about the job that each young person may take up. The section is closely linked with the self assessment and self knowledge included in other parts of the programme.

Health and hygiene   Much of the total programme can be regarded as 'health education'; this section would be more especially about health and hygiene. In most secondary schools some of the information included in subject areas contributes to health education, and it is important that there should be some co-ordination of effort in this respect.

Personal interests   This would be about pursuits and leisure interests that young people can follow outside school, especially those that can be continued after leaving school. Here also, there will be a need for liaison with other departments in the school.

Year by year   The young person's natural development during the five years of secondary schooling, together with the routine of the school, would suggest certain points of emphasis year by year.

First year   The change from junior to secondary school can be quite dramatic, from a close, familiar and often small setting, to a larger, mobile and sometimes more impersonal regime. Many young people can take this change in their stride, but others find it daunting and unsettling, and to some it can be quite traumatic. It is vital that the new entrants should be helped to feel at home within the first few hours of their coming into the school. Most schools recognize the importance of an induction programme, and give time for it. It is likely that the first-year programme will in general be somewhat inward looking, with special emphasis on building a supportive and caring situation within the pastoral group.

Second year   There is a danger that second year pupils can feel themselves as of no particular moment in the school. Secondary school is no longer new, and there may be no obvious points of emphasis to be expressed through the pastoral programme. It is, therefore, especially important that efforts should be made to retain the second-year pupils' identification with the school – for example through year events. It would also be appropriate for the second-year programme to be more outward looking. At least the programme must be vigorous in engaging both the participation and the increasing responsibility of the second-year pupil.

In some schools there is a significant break between the second and third year, which may even involve a move to a different site or part of the campus. If this is the case, then an induction programme should be mounted that settles the young people into this phase of school life, and established the pastoral group as a caring community.

Third year   In many schools there is considerable attention given during the third year to the beginning of careers education, and to the choice of the subjects that the student will take into their fourth- and fifth-year studies and examinations. 'Careers education' at this stage needs to be a truly educational experience, helping young people to inform themselves about the adult world of work. Otherwise each student may merely focus on a limited range of careers that would be of interest to him or her, and switch off during the remainder of the programme. The self-assessment and self-knowledge that run through the pastoral programme are an essential preparation for careers guidance.

In approaching the choice of subjects in readiness for the fourth-year academic programme, there should be a good deal of emphasis on the student's personal planning and efforts in study. It is especially important that they should be encouraged to keep their doors open.

Fourth year   In many schools students settle down at the beginning of the fourth year to the study programme for the final two-year run-up to public examinations, and it is important that there should be a good deal of mutual support for this with the tutorial groups. This is also an extremely important year in so many young people's social and emotional development. Adjustment is taking place, with a change in identity from child to young adult. Since personal movement is inevitable, it is an especially fruitful time for some concentration on the deeper issues of personal development. In the fifth year there will be much less opportunity for this, since sights will be kept fairly closely on the preparation for examinations.

Fifth year   The main concern for many young people in their fifth year will be their performance in the public examinations which they face at the end of the year. Considerable attention will need to be given in the pastoral programme to the support of academic effort. At the same time many young people will be at the threshold of leaving school and entering the adult world of work, and it is vital that they should be helped to gain the skills and assurance to face that step. The social skills involved will have been built up steadily during the five years, but when faced by the immediate prospect of leaving school, they are likely to assume a greater urgency.

The tertiary stage   There is a most urgent need for support and personal development programmes for this stage, whether it be in sixth form, in tertiary college, or technical institution. An appropriate induction programme is required to focus on both social and academic issues. A continuing programme is also required to help young people use their time profitably and economically, to develop their skills of scholarship, and to cope with personal experiences and responsibilities as they arise.

Treatment of themes

Each theme has its own importance at every stage of development through the secondary school. For example, friendship is a vital experience at every age, and the programme must return to the topic each year. However, it is important that the treatment should be cyclical rather than circular, so that the topic is treated with growing sophistication year by year.

It is important also that there should be sustained continuity. Threads need to be developed from week to week, from term to term and from year to year. To focus on only one example of this: the development of conversation skills involves the formulation of frameworks and agendas, and this will begin on the very first day. These skills will be used in the preparation of enquiries, leading to report sessions involving public statements to the whole group. In the second year, these skills in formulating frameworks and agendas can be taken further and used more formally for year meetings and other forms of public statement. The skill of formulating frameworks can later be reversed in the practice of notetaking. All these skills can be practised intensively in the third-year subject choices and careers education programme, and will finally play an important part in revision techniques and the preparation for examinations.

There needs to be some discussion about what is appropriate to the pastoral programme, and to the subject areas. Pastoral time is short and precious, and one would wish to avoid issues that might properly be dealt with in the normal subject programmes. The pastoral programme is especially about attitudes and affective issues, anxieties and personal objectives. There are also some essential skills that enter every lesson but may not be the direct concern of any. These general skills – conversations and other oral communication may be among them – can be coped with in the pastoral programme.

Approaches as content

Because pastoral work is about affective issues, so much depends upon the approach. It is the *experience* reaching young people that forms the basis of the programme, and experience arises out of the approach even more than out of the content. In fact, in this work, the approach is an important part of the content. We should not put too much faith in the impact of information on attitudes – some really potent experiences may be required to bring young people to a re-examination of attitudes. And the force of personal discovery is so much stronger than being told.

It is also important to see that a programme is educative and developmental as distinct from being problem- or crisis-based. Our aims should be to help young people to build up their own social competence, understanding and resources so that they can cope with life's problems as they arise. There is a case for individual counselling in school, but that is not a model that fits the role of the tutor responsible for a fairly large pastoral group.

Besides, there are many areas of experience for which the young people need a supportive group for personal exploration and practice. For example, in considering friendships and other peer relationships – a key to so much else in life – a supportive group of peers is required to enable the young person to inform him or herself about how he approaches other people, and to practise new styles of behaviour if he feels this would be helpful. Similarly, the young person in a fixed role – the class clown, for example – may very well be held to this role by the expectation of those around him. If he would like to modify his role – and we find this frequently – a group of people with whom he is in regular contact can help him to explore his customary behaviour, and the part that they play in keeping him to the role, and can release him from that pressure so that he has room for manoeuvre. They can then go to help him develop alternative repertoires of behaviour.

For this purpose the tutor is less of the overall provider than he or she may feel when teaching a subject. He is much more a third party, enabling the whole group to develop their capacity for helping one another. To some degree, the tutor will be making caring for one another legitimate, but it is likely also that the young people will need some help in learning how to help one another. This means that the quality of the experience for the young people is strongly bound up with the style of leadership offered by the tutor. There is always a dilemma. We are anxious that young people will develop their own self reliance, and yet to do so they may need to be introduced to important and challenging experiences, some of which, often those that will be most beneficial to them, they might naturally avoid.

There is sometimes some confusion about this in the minds of teachers, and when they wish to be less directive, they tend to be less active. In fact, when we are encouraging young people to take a greater level of personal responsibility, our leadership may need to be most vigorous. It is important that we should not confuse vigorous leadership with directive or authoritarian leadership. We can be vigorous by encouraging, questioning, challenging, consulting, sharing responsibility, and actively seeking collaboration.

Some techniques

Role-play

It is in some of the techniques used in pastoral programmes that the work approaches most nearly to that of the drama teacher. (For a fuller description of role-play and other techniques, see Button 1981.) But the parallel may not be as exact as would at first appear.

For example, role-play is used a great deal in this work. It is used to explore personal behaviour, group behaviour, to consider alternative behaviours, to practise new approaches, and rehearse action both in and out of the group. In each case it is enacting a personal reality, not an arranged scene. It is used in a sequence and spontaneously, whenever, for example, we can say – 'Show us what happened', or 'Show us what you mean', or 'Show us how you see it happening'. Sometimes it may amount to no more than a few minutes movement, but it may be enough to lead into a close discussion. In fact, role-play is often activated discussion. And it will be used within a conceptual framework of steps in personal development, as one of the techniques available to reach the next step.

It is important that the skills of using role-play should be at the finger-tips of every tutor, and should not be seen as the speciality of the drama teacher. It would probably be wise not to bring in a drama teacher in order to demonstrate role-play at, for example, a staff training workshop, lest the idea be put abroad that this is something difficult and the preserve of the specialist.

Support and trust exercises

Similarly with trust exercises, without a supportive spirit within the group, we shall achieve very little, so we are forever searching for ways of illustrating, in a concrete and physical way, abstract concepts like trust, caring and support. We may do this with a trust walk. Working in pairs, one will close his eyes, and the other will lead his or her partner around the room. Much depends upon the 'production' of the event, and we usually deepen the experience step by step. The objective will be to focus on caring and support, trusting and being trustworthy, not as a self-contained exercise but in order to lead immediately to other parts of the programme for which support is vital.

Other support exercises will include rocking in twos and threes, and body support. 'Body support', requires a group of seven or eight, who form a close circle with one of the group in the centre. The person in the centre will keep his or her body straight but otherwise relaxed, whilst the rest of the group first of all pivot the 'body' around the circle, passing him from one pair of hands to the next, and then they raise him or her horizontally to chest height and rock gently backwards and forwards, gradually lowering him until he gently touches the ground.

Body support links with self-feelings as well as with support. Some people have self-doubts that seem to be embedded in the feelings that they have about their body image, which sometimes surface and become identified for the very first time as a result of the exercise. This will illustrate again how the exercise is used in a context and sequence.

Communication skills

The development of communication skills is an illustration of the way

70

in which a sequence and steady build-up of experience and expertise needs to be maintained, especially when vital experience can be planned as a by-product of another main theme. Sometimes the activity will be a direct exercise in communication, but other activities, for example an action research programme about other people in the community, will be so designed to offer practice in skills that have been initiated by previous activities.

In the early stages there needs to be a good deal of emphasis on listening, especially when young people are in the habit of talking over one another. The construction of agendas or frameworks is a key concept in developing the skills of sustained conversation or the formulation of enquiries. By this is meant a series of prompts or directions in which the conversation that the young person has prepared in advance, may go. At the beginning this can lead to fairly mechanical prompting or questions, but the skill rapidly grows and the conversations soon become much more organic. In fact the ability in oral communication can grow so rapidly, that one wonders why so many young people leave school still seriously inarticulate.

The skill of constructing agendas or frameworks can be used in so many ways – not only in conversations, but also in preparing to receive visitors, preparing enquiries and action research, in frameworks for public statements, and for the preparation of essays and ultimately examinations. This is one of the ways in which skills that are central to pastoral concerns have a direct contribution to make to the academic work of the students.

In the pastoral context, communication skills underlie caring, concern and interest in the other person, and in this, empathy plays an important part. It is possible to focus directly on empathy through simple exercises, but at a more sophisticated level it enters all the attempts to understand the other person's position. Role-play can often make a very important contribution to this.

Communication skills can be extended in a variety of ways. For example, it is possible to help young people to venture statements to the whole class or to bigger groups including strangers. I have already referred to this as 'public statements'. In class teaching we so often hope that young people will contribute to the work by speaking up in class, and yet we find that so many children will avoid doing so if at all possible. Young people, even the more timid souls, can be helped to speak out in the open, as long as they are able to practise step-by-step, and are being encouraged and supported by a group of peers. There are great opportunities for this, especially when conducting programmes through Socratic group discussion.

Verbal communication is of course only part of the story, and it is possible to help young people to be aware of and sensitive to the subtle communication that takes place through the tone of speech, gesture, facial expression, general body language and physical contact. This can be approached directly through communication workshops, but is also inherent in so much of the exploration of individual behaviour and role-play. Spontaneity is closely associated with communication, and can be approached through spontaneity workshops. Spontaneity enters into a good deal of life, especially into relationships. To respond to other people's moods and positions demands spontaneity; so many of the difficulties that people face with their relationships arise from stereotyped responses and the lack of spontaneity.

Visitors

In the programmes with which I have been concerned, we have come to use the 'visitor technique' very extensively. By this I mean that a group will invite and prepare to receive a visitor. The initiative for receiving a visitor, for holding him or her in sustained conversation, and in concluding the occasion gracefully, will be with the young people. But the tutor will help them to prepare – and may need to challenge them very strongly to do so adequately. An agenda will be prepared, and the occasion will be carefully rehearsed through role-play.

This is a powerful experience, often for the visitor as well as for the young people. How should the young people lead into a conversation indicating a personal interest in the visitor? (Young people's recordings of these events have shown that so many of them have come to see teachers for the first time as real people – 'Previously I have seen them as teachers'). How will they greet the adult? Who will bring the visitor into the group, and how will the introductions be made? The question, 'Who will bring in the visitor?' is likely to engage the bolder spirits, but in a caring group, the slightly different question: 'Who should have the experience of bringing in the visitor?' may produce a quite different reaction.

Once established, the visitor technique can be used for all kinds of purposes. For example, think of those outside speakers brought into school who sometimes suffer switched-off audiences of young people.

Put the initiative into the hands of the young people because they need to have a conversation with that person as part of their on-going programme. And so a health specialist or a careers informant is invited, and the young people hold the initiative in their hands. Much of the purpose of the visit will already have been achieved as they prepare their agenda. The by-products of the exercise can be considerable in terms of coping with strangers and adults, including people seen in authority, coming to know others as real people and not only as functionaries, being led into thinking about responsibilities outside the classroom, and not least in encounters with the hierarchy of the school.

Socratic group discussion

There is not space within this chapter to describe in detail the techniques of Socratic group discussion (see Button 1981). It is a simple way of engaging a whole class in close discussion, and having everyone working all the time. The group is broken into threes or not more than fours, and questions are fed to the small groups for a few minutes' discussion, leading to open exchanges between the groups. The effect can be quite dramatic. A group of thirty people who have failed to maintain an open discussion, may, after a few minutes' discussion in small groups, experience really lively open exchanges. With a little thought and skill it is possible to engage even the more timid young people in open statements.

In order to prepare for the discussion, the tutor will need to foresee a sequential agenda, points for discussion which small groups can manage in only a few minutes. It is important that the jumps are kept small – the groups need to be able to cope with the next questions as a result of the open discussion that preceded it. The process is Socratic in that a question is set, which stimulates answers, which in turn form the basis for the next question. But in this case it is Socratic *group* discussion. The questions are set to small groups, the tutor engages the groups in an open exchange, and his summary of the responses from the groups forms the platform for the next question addressed to the small groups.

The skills of Socratic group discussion are key to a number of other areas of work. For example, the skill of working through small working parties can be learnt rapidly from Socratic group discussion, and deliberate steps can be taken to help the small groups to learn how to support one another in their work. Small groups can be used as personal support groups, so that many more individual young people can have a hearing from their peers than will be possible by working all the time through the total tutorial group. By calling for exchanges between the small support groups, matters that do need to be considered by the whole group can be brought into the open.

Similarly, small academic support groups can be formed, who have the responsibility for hearing from one another about each individual's progress with school work, helping one another to work out personal objectives and strategies, and encouraging one another to see the action through.

The feeling for working parties can help the tutorial group take an increasing responsibility for its own affairs. For example, many tutors have encouraged a 'caring' group, who monitor absences and illness, and make sure that the total group takes any action required. A similar group can be set up to cope with any routine administration that the tutor can share with the young people. This will increase the sense that the group belongs to the young people and is not just the teacher's group. The same spirit will inspire the appointment of a small group of representatives to, say, a year meeting to arrange some year function, as for example, a third-year careers convention.

Other approaches

The pastoral programme will need to be backed by a range of supporting papers, which may vary from papers to be used by individual young people, to detailed suggestions for the tutor. Self-assessment will be a recurring theme: for example, about social skills, role behaviour, self-feelings, and academic attainment and practice. It is most important that the emphasis is on exploration, and a series of worksheets to be completed by young people should be avoided. We are working through support groups, and the papers should be points of entry to sophisticated discussion that explore the subtleties that no ready-made paper could possibly reach.

Theoretical framework

Without a clear framework the whole programme will be at best hit and miss. The approaches and techniques are a means of reaching levels of personal understanding. There needs to be a sequence in the approach, so that each new piece of material can in turn form a basis from which the next piece of exploration can begin. This means that the tutors must be clear about a number of theoretical concepts, in order to help the young people to develop real understanding out of the experiences that the pastoral programme brings to them.

There are some obvious broad areas of understanding necessary that can be stated simply, but the subtleties that surround them are considerable. (Button 1974, 1981)

What kind of relationships do we strike, and how do we surround ourselves by other people? What does our life space look like? How far is the pattern of our life space a self portrait that we are pleased to live with?

What do we mean by friendship, and what are the skills and impediments to friendship-making?

In what ways are sexual relationships similar to or different from other relationships, and what are our responsibilities to our sexual partners?

What is our personal resilience to criticism, hostility and frustration? How well do we cope with conflict?

What are our personal feelings about authority, and how do we cope with authority figures?

How do we present ourselves to other people, how do they respond, and do we take characteristic roles? Some understanding of personal roles is important, because some young people are trapped in stereotyped and unhelpful roles. How can we help young people to release one another from unhelpful roles?

What are our own self-feelings? Self-feelings have a powerful influence on our behaviour and we need to have insights that will enable us to help young people first, to recognize their self feelings, and second, if necessary to modify some that may be acting as an impediment to them.

The effectiveness of pastoral work does not rest only on the individual's performance within this rather special support group, but rather on his or her performance in the real world outside. How are we to ensure that everything we initiate within the group will be practised in the real world outside?

How do we ensure that the pastoral programme is leading directly and persistently to collaboration between school and home? The parents, as well as the young people, are coping with adolescent adjustment. How can we help young people to play a creative part in family relationships?

How do we help young people to make a concerned contribution to the larger community outside and beyond school? It is not only a matter of attitudes and good intention: they will need the skills required to engage other people, and to take their place in community organizations.

Staff training and support

In asking teachers to carry through an effective pastoral programme, we may be requiring a style and stance that is different from their normal teaching experience. The tutor must bring the young people into a collaborative position, which is far removed from some of the dependence and passivity that can be seen in school. It may involve the teacher in a different style of leadership, vigorous but not directive, actively encouraging young people to face new experiences and share the responsibility for what takes place. The drama teacher may already have crossed a number of these boundaries, but from my experience I would suggest that we should not under-estimate the movement that we are asking teachers to make. I can also, from personal experience, vouch for the pleasure, indeed the excitement, that teachers feel as they engage young people in programmes of this kind.

It is most important that teachers are offered opportunities for in-service training to prepare for this work. But pause to consider the extent of the task. The majority of the teachers in most schools are engaged in pastoral work, and it is most unlikely that this proportion of teachers would all be either able or willing to follow external training courses. Besides, there will need to be strategies within the school as a whole for implementing the school's pastoral policy.

It is very difficult for individual members of staff to pursue a programme of this kind in isolation. Decisions are needed at management team and whole staff level to engage in a pastoral programme that will demand some preparation on the part of most of the staff. It is also difficult to implement a new and demanding programme throughout the school in one step, and most schools would be unwise to attempt it. When introducing something new there must be a pilot project, which is monitored and reported to the staff as a whole. It would be much wiser to proceed year by year, which could well involve six, ten or even fifteen tutors in a year team according to the size of the school. And for the pilot, some self-selection of tutors could be helpful.

In the action research project with which I have been concerned, we have worked through local education authorities who have established their own local training teams. Individual schools have been recruited into the programme, and each participatory school has been represented, on a substantial in-service training programme, by two carefully selected members of staff. These school representatives have first trained themselves to work with young people and then they have trained as trainers. They will be the prime-movers in the schools and will lead year teams of tutors into the programme. Support is vital. The year team becomes not only a training group, but also an ongoing support group.

It is interesting to observe the change in the role of the year head as the programme develops. Only too often the year head, if he or she is seen as pastoral head, can be swamped by referrals from the form teachers. However much they would like their role to be a kindly, helpful function, they frequently find that their energy is devoted to correction or even punishment. Within the kind of pastoral programme that I have described, behavioural problems are seen more clearly as being the concern of the tutorial group, not only of the tutor but also of the young people themselves. The year head becomes much more able to perform his or her major function as leader and support of a team of tutors. The spirit of an open and supportive regime produced by the programme makes mutual help much more appropriate and acceptable.

The rewards

Those who are responsible for pastoral work should not be diffident about making demands for time on the timetable. The prizes are very great. Young people are not free to give themselves to study if they are unsettled in their relationships or are at odds with themselves. And only too many young people are time-serving at school because they lack an identification with the school regime. If we consider the proportion of possible effort that we are drawing from the young people, it must become clear that most of them could give themselves more vigorously to their studies, and would do so if they found themselves more at the centre of their own learning. They can make demands upon themselves and upon one another that teachers would be hesitant to make.

There may even be group controls operating among students which limit effort. The 'swat' may be ridiculed, and to be too keen may be frowned upon by peers. This even happens with university students. Unfortunately, as tutors we can be caught up with these group controls or 'group norms', without clear strategies, or time and occasion to deal with them. This is one of the issues appropriate to the pastoral programme, and is one of the reasons also that teachers need help and training to see it through.

In these ways the pastoral programme can add very materially to the effectiveness of the remainder of the school day. For certain skills, for example skills of conversation and the preparation of frameworks and agendas, the pastoral programme can serve as an ideal medium. And the rewards are not all with the young people: the by-product in staff security and development can be very real.

PART TWO

Teaching Strategies

4 Drama and language development

Peter Chilver

Over the past ten years or so, drama has tentatively (some would say, precariously) established itself as part of the school curriculum. It has done this partly as a subject in its own right, with its own specialist teachers and its own examination syllabuses, and partly as a subject related to and taught alongside a limited number of other subjects, usually English, movement and dance.

In this essay I wish to argue that the next step in the use of drama in education is its recognition as an essential part of language development right across the curriculum. In other words, it is time that we asserted that not only is there a *subject* called drama, but also that there is an *activity* called drama, which is part of virtually every subject that is taught in schools.

This involves the exploration of three different, but related questions:

What is meant by drama across the curriculum?

How does drama (across the curriculum) promote language development?

What is the teacher's role? or, more precisely, what kinds of activities does the teacher of, say, science or geography, need to be able to initiate in order to use a dramatic method within his or her subject?

What follows is an introductory attempt to answer these questions.

What is drama across the curriculum?

Drama is about people interacting with each other. It is a form of thinking employed not only by dramatic artists who write plays and

81

make films (for example) in which they seek to capture the living experience of people interacting with people, but also by people in the everyday world. Whenever we work out how we will behave (or have already behaved) in a given situation we are to some extent thinking dramatically. The same is true when we actually enter into the situation, as when we present ourselves for interview at the personnel office or for trial at the Old Bailey. At such times we are not merely dramatists, we are more precisely improvising dramatists, working within the confines of a highly organized and ritualized framework or structure.

Drama as an autonomous subject in the school curriculum has its roots, but not necessarily its aims, in the various forms of dramatic art. Drama as an activity for use right across the school curriculum has its roots in the various ways in which we use drama in the everyday world.

What is meant, though, by talking of drama *as an activity*? Drama is an activity in the sense that reading, writing and talking are also activities. They are all ways of thinking overtly and purposefully. They are all activities, too, which until very recently were seen as the exclusive province either of specific subjects in the school curriculum or of specific stages in education. In general, reading was something to be taught in the elementary school; writing was something to be taught by the English teacher; and talking was something that needed no teaching at all. The 'language across the curriculum' movement is slowly changing this, with teachers beginning to accept and explore their roles as teachers not only of their subjects but also of the activities which are inherent in their subjects. Thus the science teacher thinks not merely of imparting a body of knowledge but also of helping children to read science, to write science and to talk it.

Drama, like reading and writing, has suffered neglect because it has been seen as exclusively a specialist activity. But the geographer is as much a dramatist as he or she is a reader or writer or talker. So, too, is the scientist or economist, the historian or sociologist.

A good example is afforded by the study of the law – something which figures however briefly in most social studies courses for children in their early adolescence. It also is increasingly popular as a subject in its own right for later stages of secondary and of tertiary education. The study of the law is partly a matter of reading, writing and talking about decisions of the courts and of parliaments, and the often complex interaction of the two. But it is exceedingly difficult to understand either of these – whether law court or parliament – without also understanding the processes by which both of them work and function. And one of the best ways of understanding them is to 'act out' these processes in some hypothetical context. Thus lawyers have long employed the 'law moot' or mock-trial as an important part of their training.

In effect, then, one aspect of teaching any subject is that of introducing the learner to the various activities in which that subject is *employed*, so that the learner becomes experienced in making all those decisions which, in real life, are based on the specialized knowledge of that particular subject. Thus the child studying geography begins to explore the work of the geographer as an adviser to town-planning committees, or the child studying biology becomes involved in the simulated work of, say, a pressure group concerned with some aspect of public health. Or the student-economist explores problems of investment as the member of a board of directors.

A second aspect of teaching any subject is that of introducing the learner to those activities which the subject is *concerned with* (and not necessarily employed in). History is at least in part about the drama of public affairs, about decisions to declare war and peace, about conferences and congresses, about revolutions and cabals. The simulation of such activities, with varying degrees of closeness to the complexities of real life, is again a very important and instructive part of learning such subjects. And this is the principle involved in the use of improvised drama as a way of studying a literary text. One way of coming to understand why Shylock behaves as he does, is by acting out the problems with which he is confronted and seeing how close one comes, and why, to the decisions made by Shylock himself.

Drama, then, is an activity. To be more precise, as a part of teaching and learning in the classroom it can be thought of as *three separate kinds of activity*, each of which is a variation on the other two.

To begin with the simplest, there is the dramatic activity where *one person assumes a role* in order to be questioned or interviewed by the others. An example is when someone, whether pupil or teacher, assumes the role of Alexander Fleming in a science lesson in order to hold a press conference for interested but uninformed journalists just after his discovery of penicillin. There is, of course, an element of role play for everyone else (i.e. for those playing the journalists) but in this particular kind of drama their involvement and hence their role-play can be minimal.

83

Second, there is the dramatic activity where *a pair or a small group assume related roles* in order to act out some kind of encounter, as when Elizabeth I meets with her counsellors to debate the case for and against executing Mary, Queen of Scots. An example from a quite different subject would be a group of mathematicians coming together to advise an insurance company as to which of a number of people's lives are worth insuring, and why.

And there is finally the dramatic activity where *the whole class, working together, assume related roles*, again in order to act out some kind of encounter, as when a conference of natural scientists is called to examine Darwin's theory of evolution, perhaps to be joined by representatives of other 'concerned' and contemporary sectors of the community, such as the Church and the press. This is the most complex of the three activities in that the participants must all have a certain amount of information, knowledge and motivation which is specific to them individually and is not known to the others. Failing this, there is none of the element of surprise, of having literally to improvise in the face of the unexpected, which characterizes the real-life situation and which, therefore, needs to be present in any simulation. Setting up such an activity is quite a sophisticated business, though once teachers start doing so, children are often able to follow suit.

It is worth adding that there is a fourth and possibly more complex (in organizational terms) dramatic activity which consists of bringing together all the three activities I have just outlined, perhaps in order to create some kind of scripted or finished production to be shown to an audience. An excellent example of this in the work of a class is offered by Elyse Dodgson's essay in this book. It is also a way of working which has long had, and continues to have, an interesting place in the professional theatre, and in the cinema and television.

How does drama promote language development across the curriculum?

Many of the proponents of drama in education have emphasized its role in promoting social and emotional development. For present purposes I wish to leave this aspect of dramatic activity to one side – not because it is unimportant, but rather because the teacher of other subjects, such as science or mathematics, is likely to look elsewhere to justify its inclusion in the classroom. Thus, how does dramatic activity help someone to master the intricacies of science or economics? and so to further the learner's language development as a scientist or economist?

Three factors can be present in dramatic play, each of which can make a significant contribution to the players' understanding. First, the participants are indeed playing, and hence to some extent uninhibited by what they do or do not know; and it is even possible, and at times very useful, to play at knowing less than one knows and at knowing more than one knows. Second, the participants are playing together, and hence able to share ideas and develop them together. And third, the players can constantly return to the subject or topic itself for further support and inspiration.

These factors together give enormous scope for the development of language and learning:

they stimulate the opening out of a subject or field of enquiry;
they reveal very cleary the assumptions being made by the learners;
they provide opportunities for shared problem-solving.

Opening out the field of enquiry

Here are a class of 12-year-olds who have spent several sessions studying the work of Galileo. One of them now opts to be Galileo and to be interviewed by the rest of the class as if they are members of a papal committee set up to investigate his thinking. Here are some of the questions that are put to him:

What is a star?

What is a planet?

Why did you try to prove your theory?

I can't quite understand that. Could you explain that again?

What does magnify mean?

What is a telescope?

Why do you want to prove your religion is wrong?

What makes the Earth move?

Can you see the Earth move?

Where do you get all these mysterious words from?

Each question is followed by extensive discussion and requests for further clarification. But what is especially valuable is the chance to use the context of play as a vehicle for going over ground that has already been covered, and in effect see if it really does, after all, make sense. One could say that this kind of activity allows the learner to articulate his or her knowledge, doubts, and uncertainties. It takes the subject of study out of the specific context in which it has been studied so far and allows the learner to relate the new to the familiar, the familiar to the new.

Revealing the learners' assumptions

Because dramatic play has this capacity to open out the territory across which we are thinking, it also reveals quite clearly the assumptions which the players are making, and the gaps and the misconceptions in their thinking. It reveals this to the teacher and also, very often, to the children themselves.

An illustration is offered by the work of the class of 12-year-olds just mentioned, investigating the career and ideas of Galileo. In a later session, this interchange occurs:

Pupil 1: (*As* **Pope**) You said the Earth moves round the Sun, but surely if the Earth moves round the Sun we would not be sitting here. We can't see anything moving. We would fall off!

Pupil 2: (*As* **Galileo**) We don't fall off because of gravity!

Pupil 1: But what is gravity?

Pupil 2: Gravity is a kind of force that holds the air in and holds us all here. It is a force pulling us all down. . . .

The group now break out of the drama to refute the suggestion that Galileo would have used gravity as part of his argument, since gravity is associated with Newton and he lived later than Galileo. This is followed in turn by discussion as to who lived when, and it transpires that the boy playing Galileo has little idea as to the point in history when Galileo lived. There is then a long digression to illustrate, in effects, the key scientific discoveries of the last 500 years or so! The same pupil then comments:

Galileo must have thought of something like gravity, for how else are we going round the sun? Must be some kind of force behind it. He must have thought about it.

Later, the teacher devotes a lot of time to the boy's assertion – 'He must have thought about it' – with the aim of helping to clarify the specific ways in which Galileo did in fact think out and advance his ideas. Thus the motivation for this later work arose out of the dramatic activity which pin-pointed the learner's problem for the learner himself. Here dramatic play flowed very naturally into further reading and discussion.

Shared problem-solving

Dramatic play provides immense scope for shared problem-solving, for literally acting out, here and now, in the present tense, various ways in which dilemmas and disputes can be, or cannot be, resolved.

In the following example a class of 12-year-olds have been studying the conquest of Peru by the Spanish Conquistadors. They are now looking especially at the question: How did Pizarro persuade the King and his advisers to give his project their blessing and support? The teacher asks them to work out, in small groups, some of the things which the Spanish government would expect to gain from the project, and some of the things it would fear to lose. Each group then dramatizes the scene:

Pupil 1: (*As* **Pizarro**) All you need to do is trust Pizarro. We will get the gold for you.

Pupil 2: But it still isn't right!

Pupil 1: But Spain needs the gold. And if we don't go and take it, then the Queen of England, she will soon know about it, and her men will go and take it for her.

Pupil 3: That's true. That's fair enough.

Pupil 4: How many men will you take with you?

Pupil 1: The Spaniards make a very strong army. I should think about two hundred men.

Pupil 4: Two hundred?

Pupil 1: You must remember that these people are only farmers. They're not big strong brave Spanish soldiers.

Pupil 4: Most of us are farmers, but we've still got an army, ain't we!

Pupil 2: So you say you need two hundred men. And how many are there in their civilization?

Pupil 1: Well, I need an army of –

Pupil 2: I said how many in their civilization?

87

Pupil 1: A million, maybe.

Pupil 3: Two hundred against a million?

Pupil 1: But they're uncivilized. They've got no weapons. No guns.

Pupil 4: But they've more men! Two hundred against a million!

Pupil 2: What exactly do you need, Pizarro?

Pupil 1: A few ships, to bring back the gold. And men, guns, food and clothing.

Pupil 2: This will cost quite a lot of money!

Pupil 3: But the gold will be worth a fortune.

Pupil 4: We do not want to spend this money just to get the gold. We want these people to become Christians. Don't we agree, committee?

They cover, in this short extract, a good variety of the arguments on both sides. The ethical doubts about the validity of the campaign – 'It still isn't right' – are silenced partly by the very practical consideration that rival powers will soon step in to steal this wealth for themselves, and partly by the more lofty and possibly hypocritical assertion that conquest must be accompanied by religious conversion. The practical doubts as to how so few can be expected to conquer so many are answered by the argument that a small number of civilized men, with the superior weaponry of their civilization, can easily demolish a much larger number of the uncivilized.

But not only is the problem presented in this rounded fashion, it is also explored very much as a real problem – Pizarro has to struggle to dispose of the various points raised against him. His securing of official blessing and support is not presented simply as a fact to be taken for granted, but as a problem which could be solved in a number of different ways.

In this next example, again with 12-year-olds, the children have been studying Darwin's theory of evolution. Different children are taking turns to assume the role of Darwin in a meeting with newspapermen of his time. Before doing so, the whole class have summed up what they think to be the main features of Darwin's theory of evolution:

Pupil 1: (*As* **Darwin**) Evolution takes millions of years. It is a very slow process.

Pupil 2: Absolute nonsense. The world was made in seven days and seven nights. The Bible tells us so.

Pupil 1: And some species have died out.

Pupil 3: Does God allow any living thing to die out?

Teacher: What evidence have you got that there were any species that died out? How can you prove it?

Pupil 1: For example, the dinosaurs have died out.

Pupil 2: What are they? Have you ever seen one?

Pupil 1: A dinosaur is a huge animal. More like a beast or a dragon.

Teacher: But dragons only appear in fairy-tales. What have they got to do with science?

Pupil 1: Because dinosaurs were like dragons. They lived a long time ago when we were more like ape-creatures!

Teacher: We were more like what?

At this point, the first pupil elaborates on the idea that there is evidence for man's descent from apes in the discovery, a hundred years or so ago, of the bones of prehistoric creatures who appear to be half-way between being apes and being men.

Teacher: How do you prove that these bones belong to ancestors of man? Why can't they just be the bones of some kind of ape?

Pupil 1: Because of the jaw bone and the brain. Each time the brain gets larger as the creature gets closer to being a man. Even now we could possibly be evolving. From the beginning man wanted to fly.

Teacher: But what is the reason why – how do you prove that the skulls of these ape-like creatures are the skulls of early man?

Pupil 1: Because in the beginning we have proof that man was more like an ape.

Pupil 4: But what proof?

Pupil 1: Because apes have smaller skulls than we have. These creatures have skulls that are almost like a man's but not like an ape's.

Pupil 3: This is the word of the Devil!

Pupil 1: I am a scientist, a person who investigates the past. There are scientists for different things, and I'm a naturalist. A scientist is someone who finds out the truth. More like a detective. . . .

Again what is worthwhile about the activity is the children's willingness to think out the problem for themselves, and not simply to repeat a given solution. The pupil representing Darwin makes a good shot at explaining how the prehistoric bones represent a link in the chain of evolution – a better shot, in fact, than he makes in substantiating the existence and disappearance of dinosaurs. He is handling a very complex idea, but the teacher and pupils do not let him get away lightly with his claims: 'But what proof? How do you prove? What is the reason?'

Later in the session, the teacher picks up the idea of *proving* Darwin's claims, and there is extensive discussion about how we can claim to 'know' there used to be dinosaurs, and how we can assert that man is linked with earlier ape-like creatures. The teacher also takes up another of the boy's points – 'Even now we could possibly be evolving. . . .' – and there is discussion about what this might mean, and what might be discarded as man evolves.

Drama then is a way of thinking about what we are learning, and of relating it to what we know already, and so has a valuable contribution to make to the learner's language development. It is worth emphasizing, though, that drama is not to be thought of as something separate from reading and writing and discussing. To the contrary, it belongs with these other activities – the learner advances as he or she reads and writes, and talks and dramatizes, and then reads and writes further. Nor is the contribution of drama to be taken to be self-evident. To the contrary, the teacher needs to look for evidence that the dramatic activity has promoted learning, just as one needs to when a child reads or writes or discusses. And I suggest that the same simple yardstick can be applied in each case: What range of ideas have been employed? What does this tell the teacher about the child's present difficulties? How fully has a specific problem been explored?

What is the teacher's role?

All teaching is complex, because it involves a constant balancing of priorities, some of which inevitably conflict with each other for at least some of the time. Teaching always involves tension; at its worst, the tension is distressing; at its best, exhilarating. While actually teaching the class, the teacher has to discharge four different functions, more or less simultaneously: *organize*, *observe*, *participate* and *evaluate*.

I mentioned earlier the three types of dramatic activity which are of value right across the school curriculum: where *one* person assumes a role for the whole class or group; where a pair or small *group* assume roles together; and where the whole *class* work together assuming inter-related roles. In this final section of the chapter I would like briefly to bring together the teacher's role and the specifics of teaching these different activities.

Organizing

Sessions where one member of the class assumes a role in order to talk to the rest of the class or group are the most straightforward for the teacher to organize, and hence an immensely useful and versatile aid to teaching and learning. They spring directly from reading and discussion: 'This is the problem facing Elizabeth I. This is what we know about the problem and about her. Let's give her the chance to speak for herself.' Perhaps the activity can be related to something else that is relevant, as when notes are taken at an interview with President Kennedy at the time of the Cuban missile crisis for writing up later as a newspaper report.

Group-work is set up in essentially the same way: this is the problem, this is what we know about it, now let's see how we might resolve it. Some of the most fruitful group-work is where the teacher gives separate instructions to each member of the group, thus using a smaller version of the large-scale inprovisations involving the whole class simultaneously, and where everyone has a definite and organized role. An example in *mathematics* would be a drama for two characters, a bank manager and a customer, where the customer is requesting a substantial overdraft and has the facts and figures to show how the debt will be discharged, and where the manager has fixed guidelines, laid down by the bank, for granting and not granting such a loan. An example in *natural science* would be another drama for two characters, where one is the pupil representative on the school's council, and the other is the chief cook for the school. The one is equipped with the results of a survey recently conducted in the school showing what types of foods are favoured by the children. The other is equipped with government guidelines as to the nutritional value of foods. They come together to work out a compromise list of menus for the last week of term.

In such dramas, the more carefully the basic situation is organized, the more opportunity there is to play with a wide range of ideas, and hence finally the more interesting and provocative the drama will be. At the same time, though, there has to be a balance. Too much preparation and instruction can overwhelm the players! The balance will depend, obviously, on the kinds of development the class have already achieved and in particular on their development in the subject or topic itself.

Surprise, though, is the key factor. It is essential that each character

91

has some motivation (and hence some information about what he or she wants to achieve and why) which is not known to the other characters. This means that everyone then has to think on their feet, adapting to the unexpected, as in life itself. Such information can be given to the players in written notes, or the teacher can take the players to one side and briefly talk about and explain them. These 'structured improvisations' can be devised by the teacher, or by the pupils, or can be borrowed from teachers' handbooks. Several teachers' handbooks give quite substantial examples of structured improvisations. (See, for example, Chilver 1978; Seely 1980.)

One of the continuing worries of teachers when considering any kind of group-work is how they are to set up the groups in the first instance. The more or less unanimous advice of the social psychologists is that the most effective working-groups are those which are self-chosen; are set up for a limited and very specific purpose; and where there are regular opportunities to work in groups, and in differing groups, for different purposes (Oeser *et al.* 1962; Richardson 1966). Teachers will at some times seek to bring the 'isolate' and the 'reject' into other pupils' groups, perhaps by suggestion and request, perhaps by working with such pupils themselves. At other times, it may be more useful to let them work on their own at a related activity, such as some kind of research or note-making. In fact, the more opportunities there are for group-work, the more accomplished will everyone become at working together and hence at assimilating newcomers and outsiders.

Setting up the more sophisticated exercise where everyone has a well-articulated role to play, as in a mock-parliament, or mock-trial, follows the same basic pattern, but of course with more details to organize. The range of subjects and topics that can be covered by such exercises is seemingly infinite, ranging from highly 'adult' games in the simulation of power politics to very entertaining forays into the 'whodunnit', where every child in the class has a role to play, possesses certain (and individual) important evidence, and has to be interviewed by the team of children working together as the police-detectives. One published catalogue of such simulation material includes a newspaper game, where the class assume the roles of editor, publisher, city editor, news editor, and so on, and are given all the basic materials from which to produce the next edition of their newspaper, together with clear advice as to the grounds on which they will include or exclude, accept or reject. There are also materials for an anthropological exercise, where the class assume the roles of the various members of a primitive tribe faced with a major crisis, and for similar exercises in politics, engineering, town planning and public health. (See Taylor and Walford 1972.)

Another aspect of organization is keeping of good order and discipline, so that the pupils can work usefully and productively. A couple of general principles are especially relevant to the teaching of drama. First, many disciplinary problems emanate from insufficient knowledge on the pupils' parts as to what they are supposed to be doing and why. Hence it is enormously valuable for teachers to talk with a class about the things to look for in doing the work and the things they later learn from doing it. Similarly, it is important to talk about *how* to work – the importance of sharing ideas, listening to each other, making suggestions, experimenting, daring to make mistakes, and so on. Also, work which occupies the whole class working together as a single unit (including those times where the work of a group is being looked at) enables the teacher to show models of the kind of work, and the ways of working, that he or she is seeking to encourage.

Many disciplinary problems also emanate from a lack of variety in the work expected of the class. This applies not only to variety of *subject-matter*, but also to variety of *activity* and of the mode of *organization*. In a really healthy teaching-situation there is a continual change in each of these factors in turn. For example, a good drama lesson will repeatedly lead off into discussion. Group-work will alternate with class-work. And perhaps the emphasis, especially for classes or teachers new to drama, will be upon short bursts of dramatic activity, with the class working together as a single unit.

Observing

The teacher is also an observer, noting, for example, what ideas are surfacing, what kinds of difficulties the children are finding, how they are working together, who is not involved, and what ideas are worth picking up and exploring later.

It is the teacher's observations which in their turn influence the particular decisions the teacher takes as a participant in the lesson.

Participating

The teacher can participate in a drama session in four ways. First, he or she can simply *attend to*, show interest in, the work of a group or of the whole class. This can be valuable all unto itself, for it holds up a model to the pupils of a sympathetic, interested audience – a model which otherwise many pupils might never encounter. Hence it can have a useful influence on the progress of the work.

Second, the teacher can participate by *offering suggestions and asking questions*: for example, What might happen next? What would you do if . . . ? Why not try that idea again with the players changing parts? What might have happened if . . . ? Now try the same scene at any earlier point in time . . . . What new character might now be introduced? What would happen if that character were interpreted differently? What other argument might be employed? How might that be answered? All such questioning and suggesting help to open out the pupils' thinking.

Third, the teacher can take these questions and suggestions a stage further and start teaching *'in role'* – that is to say, start acting with the children. (See Norman 1981 for a lively advocacy of 'in role' teaching and of the work of Dorothy Heathcote and Gavin Bolton; also Johnson and O'Neill 1982 on Heathcote.) There are obvious dangers in this, not the least of which is that the teacher will entirely monopolize the work and reduce the children to the status of audience or attendants at the teacher's personal psycho-drama. But the advantages are very real indeed. As the teacher takes a role, so he or she is able to introduce new ideas, to set a pattern of new thinking, to demonstrate how one actor can help another, and generally to enrich and enliven the drama. And children tend very much to enjoy the teacher's role-playing, and to respond and adapt to it. Quite often, too, it helps the teacher to see what is difficult about the situation as originally set up and to suggest changes accordingly.

It is obviously a mistake for the teacher always to work in role, and equally obviously a mistake fo the teacher always to take the 'best' role. But even the best role may usefully be taken by the teacher at certain times, especially in the early days of such activity, with the teacher, say, taking the role of Darwin when he comes to be interviewed. Equally useful, is for the teacher to join in the questioning and to use this as a way of introducing a different type of question and a different type of questioner. Similarly, it can be immensely stimulating for the teacher suddenly to introduce a new character to a drama, and in this way to illustrate to children the endless possibilities for thinking and rethinking.

The teacher's appearance 'in role' can be thought about in the same way as the teacher's role in pupils' discussion. Discretion, silence, sympathetic attentiveness and good listening all have a major part to play. But, in the same way, the teacher's interventions can be immensely useful in changing the style and direction of a discussion and in literally teaching children *how* to discuss.

In addition, the teacher participates in the work not simply by what he or she does during the drama, but also by those ways in which the drama is later *utilized*. Discussion of some of the ideas raised; exploration of 'what might happen next?'; extension of ideas into other work, such as writing and discussion and further reading; these are some of the ways in which the teacher in effect demonstrates the usefulness and importance of the work, and hence very much affects the quality of the work itself.

Evaluating

The evaluation of all classroom work, and not simply of drama, is a complex business. Even with something as seemingly fixed and tangible as a written essay, teachers' comments and interpretations are likely to differ widely. Drama, being so social and improvised, is also likely to be even more elusive. Despite this, as I have already indicated, what the teacher needs to look for is essentially simple, and essentially no different from what is to be looked for in a written essay:

1) What range of ideas have been employed and are they relevant and interesting?

2) How widely has the problem been explored? How carefully and how inventively? (For more detailed discussion of evaluating pupils' thinking, see Chilver and Gould 1982; Nixon 1981.)

3) What does this tell me about the work so far? What must be done next? What kinds of assumptions are the children making which are misleading? What gaps and errors are there in their understanding which might be usefully attended to at this stage? In other words, what kinds of reading, talking, writing and drama should come next?

It is worth adding that this same question – what should come next? – in in fact the most divisive question we could ever wish to give to any two or more teachers seeking to evaluate the same piece of work. And it becomes even more divisive when put also to parents, politicians,

95

journalists and so on. The difficulty emanates from another question: How much should the learner know about any given subject before the teacher can sensibly move the learner on to doing something else? For example, how much should the 12-year-olds who have looked at the work of Galileo actually know about Galileo before calling it a day and exploring a new topic?

In fact all learning involves exploring ideas which we can explore more fully later on when we will also have explored other ideas that are relevant. In other words, the curriculum, as Bruner has argued, is essentially spiral, with central ideas appearing and reappearing and even transforming as we learn more and return to what we already know and come to know it differently (Bruner 1966). Drama can make a major contribution to this spiral, not least because as the dramatists set to work and start building their own bridges from the new to the familiar, so they find the gaps and inconsistencies in their understanding and begin to *ask their own questions*. And these questions, because they come so spontaneously and directly from the children themselves, offer the clearest pointers to the teacher as to the next stage on the spiral: where we go from here.

5 Exploring social issues

Elyse Dodgson

The work I shall describe has all taken place at Vauxhall Manor School in south London. This is a comprehensive school of some thousand girls, the majority being of West Indian origin. The social issues that many of my pupils choose to explore are often directly related to their own experiences of being female and black; the work that is documented here is related to these themes.

It is my wish as a teacher to help my pupils to achieve a better understanding of the world they live in and to become dynamic, active people. I would like them to appreciate some of the concepts and to have the courage and conviction to deal with the social issues that are going to affect their lives. Drama can make a significant contribution; as one of my fifth-year pupils affirmed, 'It can teach you what you don't even know!'

In recent years I have become dissatisfied with many of the lessons I have taught, participated in, or observed in the area of 'exploring social issues'. Themes to do with 'isolation', 'crime', 'pollution', and even 'racism', and 'sexism' were, for me, becoming repetitive and superficial when approached primarily on the basis of subjective feeling and intuition. I have become more and more aware of the need to do research in order to introduce background material into this work. It seems to me that lessons limited to the subjective experience of pupils (including the influence of television), which do not introduce an element of fact, personal testimony and political analysis, leave us teaching pupils what they in fact already know, or think they know. We thus fail to give our pupils the tools to alter their perspective on these issues and make social change.

In my view this kind of work requires a genuine interest, by the

97

teacher, in the social issues being tackled. The quest to find relevant materials can be demanding and consuming; it needs to become a way of life, part of our own education as well as our pupils'. The criteria for choosing material may vary according to subject and focus, but it must always have the potential to be introduced effectively into the drama. I tend to choose material that falls into at least one of five categories. I underline everything I read with this in mind.

First, I make a note of any *factual material* that might help to inform the drama. In a work about the plight of migrant workers we focused on the struggle of Mexican–American farmworkers to form a union, and I was able to introduce some of the details about their pre-union conditions which I had made note of in some earlier reading on the subject:

The average farmworker lived 49 years. . . . A migrant worker's baby was twice as likely to die as babies of other people. Farmworkers are three times as likely to get hurt on the job. They were the lowest paid workers in the country. [Cantarow 1980, p. 122]

I am always looking for interesting *dilemmas*, situations that will confront my pupils with the problems which are faced or have been faced by others. For example, with one group interested in exploring the effects of contraception on the role of women, I used material I had marked from an account of working wives before the First World War, on the Lambeth streets in which many of them live:

Though fond of the children when they are there this life of stress and strain makes the women dread nothing so much as the conviction that there is to be still another baby with its inevitable consequences – more crowding, more illness, more worry, more work and less food, less strength, less time to manage with. [Reeves 1979, p. 153]

I am constantly trying to find descriptions which contain *vivid images* that might be used to heighten the drama and sometimes provide a focus for it. In an extended work on the persecution of women as witches in medieval times, it was such a description that prevailed: 'In 1585 two villages were left with only one female inhabitant each.' (Ehrenreich and English 1976, p. 24). The image of 'one living woman' influenced our whole study of the subject.

I also consider any *analysis* of a particular issue that will help to place our work in a wider context. For example, in a drama based on the condition of *anorexia nervosa* and the causes and effects upon its sufferers, it was helpful to draw links between social status and slimness. An article making this connection was useful:

For a great many women, manipulation of their own bodies is too often their only means of gaining a sense of accomplishment. [Parker and Mauger 1976, pp. 6–10]

Finally, and perhaps my most important consideration, is the use of *personal testimony*. The individual struggles, the triumphs, the frustrations, the tragedies of other people's lives are for me what becomes the real 'meat' of the drama. It is the introduction of these accounts into the lesson that engages my pupils most profoundly on an emotional level, with the knowledge that the work they are doing is based on real situations and the experiences of real people. So when a group asks to tackle some of the issues surrounding 'rape', I will include testimony from Susan Brownmiller's book *Against our Will* (1975). When they are engaged in a drama about the unemployed, I have used documents from Studs Terkel's *Hard Times* (1970), an oral history of the depression. I would also, if possible, provide them with the opportunity of meeting people whose experiences are relevant to the problems they are exploring. It is an ongoing process; there is a vast amount of material that I have gathered but never used. Sometimes I return to something I had made a note of years before and am finally rewarded with the discovery that it will serve a particular lesson of the moment well!

While I continue to emphasize the importance of finding relevant documents and accounts that will provide pupils with a richer and deeper understanding of social issues, I must stress that the experience takes place in the realm of drama. It requires constant consideration of the structure of the drama, of its conventions and the range of devices and strategies available. It is the combination of choosing appropriate materials and knowing how they might be employed within the drama form that can give our pupils a unique understanding of social issues.

The lessons I have documented were on the surface concerned with two very different areas of experience. Both, however, aimed at increasing political awareness through relating our own situation to that of others. The majority of my pupils live in the Brixton area of London. It was not surprising, therefore, that when I asked one fourth-year class if they had some particular area they wanted to pursue (when they returned from their Easter holiday in May 1981) they wholeheartedly agreed on 'something to do with the "Brixton riots" '. After further discussion it became clear that they were asking to explore this topic throughout the curriculum: a project in social studies, a taped discussion in English, accounts of their own experiences in the form period. 'How shall we approach this in drama?' I asked them. They were interested in looking at the quality of race relations within the community and the effects of 'discrimination' which many of them felt were at the root of the problem. They all agreed upon this area for their focus, but there were many conflicting feelings about the approach to this topic.

With some groups working on particular themes, I find myself constantly negotiating aesthetic distance. This class had enjoyed working on historical pieces before in order to make more sense of a current issue; they had looked at the position of women through the experience of a group of 'force-fed' suffragettes and the conditions of the unemployed through the suffering of the depression. I suggested they might want to use another historical inroad to this issue, but some were negative, others were undecided and a few wanted to keep this work firmly rooted in the present. As we were unable to agree we all made further offerings and settled on the idea of 'another country', 'another culture', 'something similar only more dramatic'.

The obvious country that came to everyone's mind was South Africa. They all knew it as a country where there was a great deal of racism, but we all felt we would begin from almost complete ignorance. Some of the girls had never heard of the word 'apartheid' and others didn't realize that Julie, who is white, would not be going to the same school as Alison, who is black, and sitting next to her in class. This produced shock and a lot of incentive to find out more. I believed this topic would certainly help them focus on many of the issues they were concerned with. It would introduce them to subject matter they had not come across before and was a topic that I myself was interested in researching further.

In an earlier chapter in this book, Gavin Bolton writes about the final drama experience meeting 'the pupils wants and the teachers intentions'. That is precisely what I hoped to do, by using their own interest as a starting point, but also by introducing subject-matter that would give them opportunity for an increased understanding. If they had rejected what I introduced, then I would have had to think again. If the material was not capable of genuinely engaging us all, then there was less likelihood that individuals would find the drama work useful.

Somehow I knew that all my personal reading over the next few weeks was going to be about South Africa. I collected articles and pamphlets and used this as an excuse to read some of the work of the South African novelist, Nadine Gordimer, which helped me soak up the atmosphere of the country. I wanted the girls to have an experience that would enable them to understand something about a person's own individual struggle against apartheid. I finally decided to concentrate on a series of incidents described in a book by Hilda Bernstein, *For Their Triumphs and for their Tears* (1978), a moving document about women's experiences in apartheid South Africa.

The incidents had to do with the pass laws and the decision of the South African government to issue pass books to women in the 1950s, a condition that was up until then only imposed upon African men. The description of these events contained a great deal of factual material about the system of apartheid. It presented us with some powerful dilemmas that would affect both black and white people living under this system, and offered us the opportunity of imagining the lives of individual women in this situation through the personal testimony given in the book. The campaign waged against these laws is depicted vividly as the most prolonged struggle by women in South Africa:

Women had reason to fear the carrying of passes, having been forced to witness all their lives the effect of the pass laws on African men: the night raids, stopping in the streets by police vans, searches, jobs lost through arrest, disappearance of men shanghaied to farms, and the prosecutions. [Bernstein 1978, p. 46]

I would use the pass books as a symbol for all that apartheid stands for; I now needed to develop a structure that would enable us to maximize the potential of the material.

The device of teacher-in-role is the one I most often employ in order to feed information into the drama. To employ this effectively I sometimes have to memorize information beforehand. In the first lesson I decided to take on the role of a protest organizer in the 'pass book campaign'. I would address a secret meeting of black and white women to inform them of the kinds of demonstration that were beginning all over the nation in response to the pass books being issued to women for the first time. In role, I could explain the significance of the pass books and how it would affect peoples' lives from a position within the drama. I could give them information about how the pass books restricted freedom of movement and choice of occupation, and in role they could respond to this information.

I told them of some of the protests that had previously taken place: silent marches, the burning of pass books, making banners, and composing songs and slogans. This was all based on the factual information in Bernstein's book; I prepared and rehearsed my speech as if working from a script. Then I asked them what this particular group of women could do that would serve as their own individual protest. The pass books were to be implemented in their areas the following week; they must prepare their own act of defiance. By doing this, I was asking the girls to prepare and rehearse a piece of theatre; I find asking pupils to make theatrical statements of this kind a useful means of giving focus to the work. It provides a powerful stimulus for moving the drama on and illustrates the very thin line I believe to exist between drama and theatre.

The girls designed and rehearsed the following protest. According to their plan, the pass books would be coming to the town by train, and they, black and white women together, would sit in a tight circle, lock hands on the train rails and try to stop the train. When they achieved this they would shout and chant the slogan they composed:

Remember all us women,
Remember what we mean,
If you will not hear us,
We will still be seen,
We won't have these pass books,
We just want to be free!

There was great involvement in the preparation of the protest; they decided to wear black arm bands as a further act of defiance. I was designated the official of the government who was to get off the train when they succeeded in stopping it. They rehearsed their demonstration over again until they were confident that it would have an impact on the officials. I told them it was to be used again as the starting-point for their next lesson.

When the lesson began I spoke of the realization of what they had done and were about to do. They had worked during previous lessons in various roles as black and white women in the anti-apartheid movement. I asked them now to set up their train tracks, which they did by putting mats on the floor. Then I asked them, before they actually took their places on the tracks, to look in the direction of the train and discuss how they felt about what they were going to do:

'I'm scared, but I have nothing to lose.'

'I'm scared, but we must all be equal in this country.'

'They have no right to stop me on the street; they will split up all the families.'

I noticed that already the girls were beginning to use information they had received in the previous lessons. The material was beginning to give them more to think about and develop in the drama. It was also beginning to extend their use of language. When they all took their places the planned protest began, and I, in role as the official, stepped out of the train, bemused, disbelieving and outraged. They continued with their chanting and I laughed at the 'silliness' of their feeble act and raged at the fact that black and white women were joining hands.

As the symbol of white South African authority I was faced with over a dozen protesting women whom I was determined to move. I decided that I would have to use the convention of imagining there were other guards who had come off the train with me. I ordered them to remove each of the women. The girls adapted to the convention and struggled with the imaginary guards until they were all seated in a police enclosure ready to be 'interviewed'.

At the police station I made it clear to them that it would not be possible for them to win and calmly showed them the pass books that I intended to issue that day. I interviewed them individually, although I allowed them to remain in the same room so they could all take part in the drama work.

Some of them tore up the pass books, others threw them on the floor, a few just refused to accept them, others tried to destroy them all. I mocked and laughed at them assuring them that I had all the power and there was plenty of time to put them in their place. I showed great contempt for a particular 'white woman' who had every advantage of a good government subsidized education. 'What kind of advantage is an education like that, when we never see a black face in our school except as a servant?' she replied. Another woman (a white pupil playing a black domestic worker) was so frightened she refused to speak; she nearly accepted the pass book but refused as the others urged her not to give up. Another white woman covered her hands with dirt she picked up from the floor and tried to blacken herself. 'Now I am black too, give me the pass book.' A wealthy white lady who belonged to a well known family (played by a black girl) raged at me for what had been done to this country that 'belongs to Africans'. I told her that even her family connections could not save her now; everything was being recorded; everything would be held against them.

In my view, it is important when working on issues to do with race to point out to pupils that they can adopt the role of a person of a different colour. Many pupils enjoy taking on the role of someone from a different racial background. In this drama, I was not sure what roles the girls had chosen, and I did not always know whether they were black or white. As this was crucial to what was happening at the police station, I was occasionally puzzled. They must have sensed this because they quickly began to give me hints:

'I live in the slum.'

'I work for a family as a servant.'

'I live in one of the homelands.'

When the interrogation finished and each one still refused a pass book, or in the case of the 'white women', 'to give up and give in', I made it clear that I had the right to detain them without trial. I'd prepared a speech, in order to give them more information about the legal system in South Africa but I was thwarted by a spontaneous stamping of feet. When I called in additional guards to break up the rebellion, the girls resumed their convention of struggling with the imaginary police, moved themselves over to the other side of the room and fell on the mats.

For a few moments there was chaos. I was sure that none of us knew where the drama was going. It was one of the pupils who thought most quickly and clarified the situation for us. She suddenly began to describe a cell that she was in, and we all realized that the mats had now become a prison cell. As a teacher, this was a very rewarding moment, because I allowed my pupil to take the reins of the drama and with confidence and imagination move it in a new direction.

In an earlier chapter, Gavin Bolton stresses the need to make children conscious of dramatic form. I believe it is precisely this awareness that enables pupils to make a valuable contribution to the meaning of the work; pupils can in this way take an active part in their own learning and in the learning of others. I feel that some of my fourth-year pupils are capable of operating the dramatic form with great skill. They consider the structure at the same time as thinking about the dilemmas which were implicit in the material we were using. As many of them informed me later, they made some of the decisions in the drama on the basis that they were 'working for more variety' within the dramatic form.

On their own in the cell, they began to express doubts that they had not before articulated in front of the police. I decided to stay out of the drama for the time being, shouting to another official, 'leave them alone for awhile; they will weaken when they are left to their own devices!' Several indicated that they wanted to give up, others tried to strengthen them with stories of the victories other women around the country had had with this protest. They described how the jails had been filled with hundreds of women, too many to be contained. Here again they referred to material that was introduced into the lesson previously.

It soon became apparent that not all the girls would have the same degree of courage to face the authorities. I informed them that they would be given one last chance to make up their minds and began to address an imaginary group of police officers: 'What is the make-up of this new breed of women, both black and white, who dare to defy the laws of our country? From what kind of experience does their courage grow? It is important for us, if we are to defeat them, that we understand this.'

I stopped the whole-group work at this point to ask them to think about the kinds of experience that might have given these women such courage. I asked them to choose an incident that might have happened to one of the protesting women, something that might have influenced their determination to establish a different kind of society. For the first time in the lesson, I was asking them to work in smaller groups and to show their work. For the first time I was giving them the opportunity of working outside the drama, and of discussing what had happened so far.

They worked in two groups and presented two different stories. One was about a white woman who was rescued from a fall by two black passers-by. She entertained them in her home afterwards and was swiftly ostracized by her neighbours. The other was the tale of a black domestic servant who was forced to work throughout a difficult pregnancy and lost her child. Her sister visited her to find her working under the same poor conditions and still refusing to believe in the death of the child. She vowed to make some changes.

Finally, I asked them to return to the cell and described to them once more their predicament. This time I added details about the conditions of the cells they would occupy, most of them in solitary confinement. Again I used descriptions taken from personal testimony that I had memorized. I advised that up until now the time had been easy for them; they were to make their decisions at once. I offered the pass books to each of them once more, indicating that by accepting the pass book they were accepting their government. Three girls accepted the pass book; the others remained condemned.

The following statement is by Alison, one of the girls who decided to accept the pass book. I asked her, shortly after the lesson, to discuss her feeling about the drama and what she had learned about the issue she had chosen to work on:

At first you could feel the tension as we all linked hands and sang the song. You could feel that we all really believed what we were doing and it was really scary when we were singing the song and held hands and closed our eyes. You could see the train coming, even though we were only playing a part and there was no train. You still felt frightened in case it didn't stop. When Simone said it stopped, we all gave a sigh of relief. Even though there was nothing, we imagined it so strongly.

The interrogation was really frightening because we were not sure what was going to happen. For me the most frightening bit was the cells. When you described it I realized I might have to live the rest of my life there and so I took the pass book; I knew I would have to accept anything that came after.

I think I would make that decision in my own life because one thing I cannot take is loneliness. When you do drama you have to take in some of the consideration of your own mind. They would have detained us indefinitely without trial. I couldn't take those conditions; it would have been forever.

I think what we found out in the drama surprised most of the girls. We heard things on television like cricketers have been blacklisted for playing in South Africa, but we never really understood what it meant and it was really surprising to learn that black people have to live in certain areas; it really did. surprise me because we didn't think that anything like that went on any-- where. Julie said she never even heard of the apartheid system. We discovered how people had to live going through that every day of their lives, not being able to go certain places, eat certain places. Sometimes when you thought of it, you just wished it was made up. It was like a shock; you never thought it could be that bad.

It made me feel that a lot more has got to be done. Like we think that our problems are bad, which they are and then we think of the black people in South Africa and their problems are even worse. Afterwards when we weren't in lessons we got together and talked about it and a lot of us were really shocked at how the people were treated and we said if we could we'd like to do something about it.

In the discussion that followed with all of the girls everyone agreed that they had been thoroughly involved in the lesson and felt they had learned a great deal about some of the issues they had an interest in and others of which they had not been aware. However, they were all dissatisfied with the way that I had ended the lesson:

'I think we should have been taken to our cells and allowed to express our feelings about it as we did in the beginning of the drama.'

'I wanted to know what happened when they returned to their cells; they may have changed their minds.'

'I wasn't quite satisfied with how it ended; that was the only disappointing part about it.'

I agreed with the girls and appreciated being told by them that I needed to structure the lesson differently, giving them more time to reflect on the implication of their decisions and to distance themselves from the intensity of the situation.

The work I describe next is on the surface less contentious, but involved the girls in making important discoveries about being female. It also uncovered some hidden feelings with regard to the mother and daughter relationship. I will try to show how the use of materials and the length of time we gave ourselves to explore this issue helped us to develop a fresh understanding; one that I would hope would contribute to the quality of these relationships in the future.

A class of fifth year girls chose this theme to work on because they were inspired by a play they saw by the two-women company *Dovetail Joint*, based on aspects of Nancy Friday's book, *My Mother, Myself* (1979). The girls decided that they wanted to use this idea as the focus for their 'presentation' for their CSE Mode 2 Examination in Drama, which must take the form of an 'anthology or thematic presentation'. The syllabus specifies that at least a half-term should be spent on preparing for this; as it was the two terms we spent on the project seemed only just adequate.

I have already mentioned how it can be difficult to separate drama from theatre. In this case I used extensive work in the drama mode to help develop what later became a theatrical presentation. I believe it is possible to create new forms of presentation that are more relevant and more appropriate to school pupils. For me this is more likely to happen when there is time to translate the drama into theatre, when the presentation becomes the natural extension of the drama work that has gone before.

I will outline some of the drama work that was used as the basis for this fifth-year presentation, *Mothers and Daughters*, with particular reference to some of the materials that were introduced.

We began with pregnancy. I worked in role as an expectant mum along with others in the group, going for my first ante-natal visit. I expressed many of my fears about the momentous change in my life that was about to take place, and through this role introduced some of the issues discussed in Ann Oakley's book, *Becoming a Mother* (1979). This book contains interviews with over sixty women before and after the birth of their first child; as soon as I began to introduce these ideas the pupils began adding their own. When they were ready I asked them to say how they felt about the changes going on in themselves. Some of the statements made at the time were later used in their presentation:

'I just think how wonderful it is to have a human being growing inside you, growing in your own blood.'

'I feel scared and frightened. I hear that it's very painful when you're giving birth and that you change a lot too.'

'All that worries me is the child; hoping that he or she will be alright.'

'My belly looks like a swollen balloon.'

'It seems strange having someone growing inside me; someone who will have to rely on me.'

'The other women say that you change. I don't want to change. I want to be me.'

We did some work about women in a maternity ward after they had given birth. Some were contented, others still confused and perplexed; some were nervous and others sinking into states of depression. I had previously introduced them to Sylvia Plath's play for radio, *Three Women* (1975 pp. 40–52) which is set in a maternity ward. In our break one girl began to look at another book I had with me, that I hadn't planned to use in that lesson. She opened up *The Lost Tradi-*

tion: Mothers and Daughters in Literature and from it extracted two lines
of a poem which suddenly became the focus for our drama:

When my mother was young
She must have been in pain
I don't remember her holding me.
[Huie in Davidson and Broner 1980, p. 261–2]

The idea was developed by the pupil who discovered the lines and
within the drama she developed the role of a mother who began to find
it very difficult to accept her baby. The various responses of the other
mothers to this woman's plight led us to a discussion about the kinds
of support that is given by the maternity services. This in turn
brought on questions about the changes that had recently taken place
in maternity care and how different this was from the past. It was then
that I decided to have another look at *Maternity: Letters from Working
Women* (Davies 1978), which contains many moving autobiographical
portraits of motherhood in the nineteenth century. I explained how
these letters were compiled. The women who wrote this book were
members of the Women's Co-operative Guild, an organization that
during the last century worked towards social reform, partly by
publishing testimonies of those in need.

I instructed the girls, as members of the guild, to get to know some
of the poor women whose experiences we were going to document in
our work on maternity. I showed them samples of letters that had
been written, which gave them an idea of the conditions they might
find. Then I asked them to work in pairs, one interviewing the other in
role so as to achieve a greater understanding of the conditions of that
time. The girls swiftly captured the extreme conditions of child birth
endured by many of these women and appeared to grasp many of the
differences between then and now. The continuous bearing of children before birth control was available, the necessity to get back on
their feet as soon as the children were born, the unhygienic conditions,
the illnesses and deaths – these were some of the issues the girls
isolated. Later they decided not to use this work in their presentation
which was to remain in a modern setting throughout. Nevertheless it
contributed to the understanding that was demonstrated when they
presented their work. The confidence the girls displayed later on was
that of people who knew they were speaking intelligently on many
aspects of the issue, both past and present.

At the beginning of one lesson I gave each girl a card and asked her

109

to write on one side what she had learned from her mother and on the reverse side something she believed she had taught her mother. This too, they incorporated into their presentation many months later.

'I have learned how to tidy and clean the house.'

'I have learned judgment, compromise and understanding.'

'I have learnt the meaning of the words "mean" and "cruel".'

'I have taught my mother to understand people my age.'

'I have taught my mother the needs of teenage girls of my generation and the understanding it takes to achieve it.'

These personal statements were written anonymously and read out, but only discussed in general terms. Clearly such material can be highly charged emotionally and must be handled with care.

I chose to develop in more detail some statements that I had compiled from a recent book on the subject, *Our Mothers' Daughters* by Judith Arcana (1979), in which she described the attempt to relate to each other as 'a terrible struggle for both women'. The girls chose several statements that they wanted to develop further through drama. They included the following:

My mother wanted me to do more with my life than she had done with hers; she felt stupid for not having continued her education. [Arcana 1979, p. 62]

My mother gets hurt easily and whenever I become more independent she becomes more hurt. [Ibid. p. 16]

I used to think when I grow up, I will not be like this. [Ibid. p. 10]

She didn't tell me anything. I was completely unprepared for life. [Ibid. p. 36]

This last statement led to a discussion about menstruation. The majority of the girls stated that they had never told their mothers when they first started their period; those that had, experienced difficulty in doing so. They chose to develop this theme by exploring the relationships in a particular family. They concentrated on an incident in which the brother in the family overhears his sister telling her friend that she has the 'curse' and runs to tell his parents, not knowing what is 'the curse'. The mother embarrassed and confused goes to her daughter's room:

Maria: Crossroads finished?
Mother: Yes.
Maria: Oh.

Mother: Maria, have you something to tell me?

Maria: No.

Mother: So what have you been telling Tracy?

Maria: I don't remember.

Mother: Are you sure?

Maria: Why, yes.

Mother: You've been telling her that you have the curse.

Maria: Who . . . yes, it's true.

Mother: And for how long now?

Maria: Few months, I don't know.

Mother: Few months and what have you been using?

Maria: I ask my friends for some.

Mother: You have borrowed from your friends! Maria you make me feel ashamed. I am your mother, whenever you have a problem you must come and tell me.

The awkwardness of the situation, the sheer inability to communicate, was something that everyone felt deeply about, and this became one of the most poignant features of the presentation.

We were not sure of the exact nature or the pattern of the work on this theme when we began, but we eventually decided to put it together in a chronological progression from pregnancy to birth, from young motherhood to difficulties with adolescent daughters, from middle to old age. I wanted, finally, to introduce them to the idea of heritage in order to emphasize the passing of time which creates the mother–daughter–mother cycle. We read a story that captured this sense of what is passed on from one generation of women to the next, Alice Walker's 'Everyday Use' from *In Love and Trouble: Stories of Black Women* (1973). The girls explored the meaning of heritage through their work in drama. I took on the role of an old grandmother, gathering her grandchildren together to tell them what she would leave to them when she died and the significance it had for her. Some responded with interest to the old woman's past; others thought the photographs, shawl and old handkerchief that I showed them were useless.

In a project such as this there was time for pupils to do a great deal of writing which they incorporated into the final presentation. They also adapted other material; it was a speech from an Apache ceremony which I presented to them as part of some American Indian material

111

on the subject that they used to create their own ceremony to finally celebrate their heritage:

Dear Brave Woman carries this girl
She carries her through long life,
She carries her to good fortune
She carries her to old age
She bears her to peaceful sleep.

Our work on the mother and daughter relationship extended over a much longer period of time than the work done with the fourth years. It was also different in its outcome, as it culminated in presentation, and the nature of the material varied. Both subject areas are, however, emotionally charged. I feel strongly that issues concerning our relationships with people must be seen in both social and political terms.

In my view, 'social issues' teaching should concern itself with areas of experience that are very close to us (for example, menstruation) and those which are at a great distance (for example, black women in South Africa). The art is to personalize areas of experience which are at a distance and to view those which are near at home in a wider context. In each series of lessons, documented in the previous pages, I started from a different end of the telescope – in the first, drama work on apartheid in South Africa helped the girls to see Brixton more clearly; in the second, drama work on their own relations with their mothers helped them to see more clearly the mother–daughter–mother cycle as their female heritage is passed from one generation to the next. Both courses of lessons are about our political understanding of situations; there is, in other words, a politics of the personal as well as of the world at large.

This work for me is only a beginning in trying to discover how the tools we have as drama teachers can best be used to explore social issues. I regret that in the past much of this work has been done in isolation. At present, I am working with other teachers to develop background materials and to find new strategies, structures and devices, within the drama form, that can improve the quality of the drama work itself, and contribute to a more profound understanding of social issues.

6 *Looking at history*

John Fines

As a teacher I am most usually employed to demonstrate teaching methods to others, sometimes students, but more usually fully-fledged teachers. I have two sorts of audience, usually: history teachers who want to know about drama, and drama teachers who want to see a teacher from another discipline using theirs. Although the audience reaction differs in many respects, one comment usually comes up whatever the circumstances: 'Ah well, you see, you are a special case, there are not many people like you, so we shall not be able to take much notice of what you have to say.'

This is an annoying comment, but it does have a grain of truth in it, and before setting out in this paper why I use drama in the teaching of history, perhaps it would be wise to set out those special circumstances. I am for half my life a scholar, devoting my attention to the personnel of the English Protestant Reformation in the period before Elizabeth came to the throne. This half of me is the dry old stick, of importance to me and a very few others; but it does mean that when I am a teacher I come from a background with strict disciplinary requirements. This other half of my life as a teacher is dominated by two factors: first I actually find deep pleasure and reward from teaching children, and secondly, I am profoundly dissatisfied with what is called 'History' in school. Thus I wish to do better, to give to children something more approaching the virtues, delights and lessons of that other side of my life, in scholarship.

The fact that I have so frequently turned to drama to do this may seem astonishing to some, and audiences often suggest that what I am doing then is expressing a strongly repressed love of the theatre. 'Were you ever a professional actor?' is a common question, and

113

frequently I am asked 'What playwright, producer or actor has influenced you most?' Well I am old enough and wise enough to know that self-analysis never works, so I don't really know whether I am a repressed actor, but I do know that apart from school plays and college reviews I have not trod the boards, and do not wish to; I think I would never make a good actor. Living in a town with a famous theatre, I only go when I have guests who wish to attend, and usually groan with boredom throughout. Frankly a sentence of no further theatre attendance for life would leave me with a broad grin on my face.

Thus when I talk of needing drama in my teaching, I am speaking of a need to make the history more historical, not more dramatic. When, as so frequently, I find children producing real drama for me, I am moved and grateful, but I often do not know what to do with it and gently shift the focus back on to history, to the grievous annoyance of my audience and probably, alas, of the children too.

Let us begin from the point of what it is I am using drama to set right – what is wrong with school history. This is best seen in the school textbook, whose aims are pretty easy to define: to simplify the vast and intractable mass of history so that pupils can cover it in the time allowed. This process of simplification leads first to a form of précis, a cutting out of as much detail as possible to leave 'the main line' clear, and a reduction of complexity on the level of understanding, whereby big issues and events, large and demanding concepts are explained in simple language and sharply patterned focus. Thus in the books the feudal system becomes a triangle, with the king at the top and the peasants at the bottom, with the nobility and clergy wedged neatly in between.

Simplification seems a noble aim in teaching, and there would be many circumstances in which one might yearn for it: if I *had* to learn to fly, for example, I might feel very grateful to an instructor who said, 'It's all simple, really, you pull back to go up, press forward to go down, and side to side for turns.' The cockpit might still be a baffling place, but at least basics would have been made clear.

But history is not a machine, nor does it have convenient basic elements or 'main lines'. My experience of history is that despite the great mass of material available, it is riddled with holes, with patches where there is no evidence to go on. It is never simple, each nostrum breaks to pieces in your hands the more you know, the more you think about it; there are no rules, no real guiding principles, and each new historian on the scene sees things differently, sometimes markedly so. History is about people trying to act in circumstances they do not thoroughly grasp because they cannot know all, and least of all can they know the future. Chance, or an unimaginable divine providence rules the world. Things that promised well turn out badly, and tragedies have heroic consequences. The attempt to explain human actions is one of the most arrogant of all our sciences.

Thus to me, simplification is the negation of history as I know it, indeed it is the complicatedness of history that is its main interest and its major message. If I can teach children that things are not as simple as they first seemed, I have, in my terms, done a good job. This may seem a negative aim, but if you consider for one moment the dangers of stereotyping, of snap answers to political problems, of easily arrived at assumptions about how society works, then the corrective power of this learning will be seen in all its glory.

And the detail *is* compulsively interesting, for it is our curiosity, our thirst for detail about other people's lives that draws us to the subject. We can't (or shouldn't) poke about in our neighbour's private letters, nor (unless by virtue of some unprincipled newshound) can we see the intimate details of the lives of the mighty; but we can when they are dead, and it is all right then. The detail that the texts omit is just the stuff which switches on the compulsive power of history. Think of all the grand design politics you had to learn about when studying Richelieu at school, and have since forgotten (because, of course, they are of no *use*); then think again of the information that Richelieu spent a half-hour every morning leaping over a vaulting horse to keep in trim. Haven't you now a little urge to see the old fellow as a human being, who might, after all be interesting? It is the detail that gives life, the simplified skeleton that illustrates dramatically only death.

Now in the context of these beliefs about history and historical education, drama, as I have come to use it, has a very rational role to play. It brings with it four cardinal virtues which I wish to discuss in this paper: first it allows one to see history as a largely unknown area in which one must experiment to find ways of understanding (whilst admitting that the understanding will never be total, never be provably true); it allows one to take history at the right pace – not the whoosh of the textbook, but the real time in which it happened, in which it was experienced; it allows one to handle issues in which the search for human motivation and the assessment of significance are clearly the main constituents of the learning – it makes the study of

115

past humanity relevant to our present concerns; finally (and possibly most importantly for me) it allows for a set of relationships in learning between teacher and pupils that I find most comfortable and condu- cive to good work – it is a natural way of doing the job.

I wish to take each of these four points and show a little of what I mean by them, and what they mean for me. I will try to illustrate each by practical examples, but space is short and anecdotes are not always the best medium of explanation. Where I use an example it is not as a proof (each teacher needs to prove everything for himself, I have found) but as a handy way of suggesting a larger meaning.

One of the commonest topics set on school syllabuses for 11- to 12-year-olds is the subject of Norman kingship. This is usually writ- ten down with an airy disregard for the complexities of the concept (which still puzzle our best professors of Medieval history in the western world) and the assumption is that there are two ways to teach it. First you can tell the children (or order them to read about) what the Norman kings did; then you write down as much as you can remember and move on to the next topic. On the other hand a keen young scholar fresh to teaching might wish to take the generalisation as a generalisation, and tell the children the major aspects of Norman kingship as an institution, and then they will write down as much as they remember and move on. Because the topic is so complex and difficult the assumption is that children cannot be operators here, they must receive and commit to memory, digest as well as they can.

Yet the topic may be explored, may be experimented with in a diversity of ways, and although the children's thought will not be at the same levels as their teachers' or their teachers' teachers, the thinking process is what we are after. In fact children have a lot of experience to bring to such a topic, if teachers will find a format in which it may be used.

I taught the subject recently and began by asking the children whether they thought Norman kings had an easy or a hard job. They discussed this question tentatively, and came to the conclusion that it depends on a lot of things about which they really didn't know very much. I sympathized with their position, and suggested that we could run an experiment to find out some more things to say about this question. In this experiment we would put a king through some of the circumstances they had mentioned, and see what happened.

So the king held a court, and we quickly discovered that it was hard to impress people and make them subject to you when in fact you needed their support and advice rather badly. At this stage the group thought the answer was 'more firmness – execute a few people, just to show.' So we went on to explore an area where firmness was needed – getting hold of money. That proved pretty difficult too, as castelan after castelan reported back with excuses as to why they couldn't pay the amount the king suggested. We then explored the getting of information – were these barons telling the king the truth, and how could we know? This involved a grand tour of the country (a large hall in which castles were scattered neatly) and the great risk of visiting one area at the expense of another. When we were in the north a rebellion broke out in the south.

What the children learned from this experimenting was that their advice to 'be more firm' was just not enough to cope with the manifold problems our poor king was facing. It became clear to them that control was in fact a relationship, and somehow the king needed to relate very closely indeed with all his barons. In the letters of complaint that flooded in at one point of our exploration, the main cry was 'We don't see enough of the King – he should bring his justice to us.'

In an hour and a half there is a limit to what one can learn about power, but this particular lesson opened up a wide range of issues that could have been followed up in relation to the Norman kings and to the study of power in general. Whether it was or not, I am not in a position to say, but two points are clear and need making: first the format chosen for the work gave the children great confidence in their power to discuss the subject and set them in a good relationship with their materials of study; second, there was no acting, no drama, such as a drama teacher might have recognized – we hadn't needed acting in order to explore the topic, we had only needed elementary roles, a willingness to take them and a willingness to use what we found as a contribution to discussion. The lesson had been a kind of very active discussion, with breaks for experimental work.

There has been a great deal of agonizing by history teachers about children's understanding of historical time, ranging from problems of knowledge of sequence ('The Anglo Saxons were followed by the Romans') to problems of understanding how time works, in great ages and periods long ago. I am not sure whether I can *understand* a century, even though I could make a stab at defining it, and I suspect that many of the arguments about understanding time are of this order; but what I would like to stress here is that work in role on particular situations can aid one to understand time as it happened, and allow people to see that minutes, seconds, hours, days and weeks had the same signification in the past as now – an important move in the understanding of historical time. Time is of the essence in understanding history, and if one doesn't get it right, then no understanding can be achieved.

Recently I had a class of 17-year-old pupils in America who were set to interpret a document detailing activity in the police station nearest to Ford's Theatre on the day of Lincoln's assassination. The two pages showed the routine activities of the station, suddenly interrupted by the big news, and lots of things happened suddenly. This 'suddenly' was the key the pupils took for their interpretation of the document, because after a short period of discussing and then accepting its authenticity, they latched on to the interesting notion that we didn't know when the desk sergeant lifted his pen and when he put it down. Now it is precisely what we *don't* know in historical evidence that requires imaginative thought, and this is where drama can help.

We replayed the document, trying to feel for the time that was hidden beneath its surface. The pupils in discussion after each fragment of replay reached for words to describe the quality of the time, not just its duration, but also its pace. They examined with some care words like 'pandemonium' to see whether they felt right in the context of the known. Various checks were possible – we noticed, for example, that in the middle of all the Lincoln material one Francis McGee was brought in – presumably just an ordinary criminal brought in by an unsuspecting officer on the beat, who couldn't have guessed what would be going on in the station. We tried to think through his reactions, and McGee's, as they pushed into history, trying to reassert normality. It was an interesting moment when two kinds of time and routine were seen commenting upon one another – the regular drunk or sneak thief, or whatever, the normal business of the station, interrupting for a moment the hugely fast pace and undirected, unusual and unexpected great assassination of a supremely important man.

The quality of the discussion on the time we were adding to the record in the document was very high, very philosophical, because we were talking about things known through experience, however vicarious that experience might be. We *could* talk about what we *had* lived through, and these students (who were undertaking a course in the arts at the time) showed me their capacity in understanding by turning the document into a musical score, adding time in the most formal way possible, during the last few minutes of the class.

In this class there had been some stronger feelings of being in the drama, because we needed those feelings in order to do the work. We had concentrated on building the police station, working out its routines and personnel, and we had tried to keep as much as we could to the known sequence, the known words and routines we found in the documents. But what we had been reaching for was not the play about the police station but an experience that would teach us more about the time element in the document we were studying. I need hardly have to add that by the end of the class, those pupils knew the document almost off by heart, without ever attempting a formal reading of it. Had I asked them at the start to read it through they would all, I am sure, have told me it was too difficult. By dipping into it, by using it as a resource, by consulting it for specific purposes, we all read it thoroughly, but not line by line, word by word. My questions had not been of the order of 'Who can read the first line?' but more of 'Does it tell us anything about what the desk sergeant was supposed to write down about an accused person?'

The third gift of drama to the history teacher is that it enables him to talk with children about the important things, rather than the trivial issues, it helps him explore types of human motivation, and helps children begin to give significance to what they are doing. So often in history teaching the learning is just received, the two elements of human motivation and significance are precisely what is lacking. Because there is no frame of understanding for the children to use, the big and important things they are suppose to learn are treated in a trivializing fashion, and the past and the people in it are simply insulted. 'The Vikings sacked Lindisfarne' the children copy out – and what does it mean? Another dreary piece of work for most, for some a gigglesome image of monks being put into bags. At least they have a laugh out of it.

Now birth and death, cruelty, despair, destruction and creation are trivialized at a cost; of course Queen Anne is dead, we all know that, and you can't hurt the dead any more, but in our failure to respect the past and see it as a way of elevating ourselves, then we fall and become mindless, throughtless, careless. If we do not respond to these great stimuli, that is one more proof of our own inability to live proper lives. Those who stultify history have a great responsibility on their shoulders.

So when I taught the Vikings recently, to a group of rather small 9-year-olds, I determined that we should come out with some understanding that would help us, make us better. I had with me a good reproduction of a Viking brooch, a work of very great beauty. I asked the children what they knew of Vikings, and they gave me the stereotype – big, rough, hairy men who went around killing, stealing and burning. That was the kind of knowledge they had, and I accepted it as such, simply commending them for their ability to dredge this information up for me. When they had given me all they knew, I put to them the paradox (and how powerful the paradox is in drama – there's a whole book to be written there): how could these wicked hateful people come to a stage when they could make an object of such beauty as this?

The children examined the brooch with care and agreed that it was an object of great beauty, and cunningly wrought. They saw the problem straight away – we must try to get an explanation, but how? When I suggested that we could experiment and produce many possible solutions, and consider them all, they heartily agreed, but clearly found a problem in seeing Vikings in their puny bodies. Luckily I had the audience there, a fairly beefy lot, so on this occasion I turned the children into directors, using the adults as their actors. The audience were told firmly that they were merely tools, and the directors warned that they would have to be pretty firm, and full of ideas. Certainly the children appreciated the role-reversal, and lived up to the situation remarkably well. One little football terracer was so lost in his work that when I quietly asked him how *they* were getting on, he just muttered out of the side of his mouth 'magic, mate – they're just magic'.

As the directors showed their work (and the actors did work very well for them) at the end, we had something like seven different explanations of how it came about that the brooch was made. There it sat glistening in the middle of the floor, and around it came evocations of the moment of its making. I found them very moving indeed, for they were all so astonishingly different, ranging from the fierce to the gentle. One group were melting down treasure when a girl said 'No, this Anglo-Saxon brooch is too beautiful to melt' and the leader roughly took it and cast it into the pot, saying 'We can do better' and was then fixed to do so. Another group at an opposite pole discovered the division of labour, all working extra hard in order to support the one artist in the group.

This power to see a multitude of explanations, to consider them from the point of view of human motivation, and to go away enriched in all sorts of ways is a power I bid for constantly as a teacher. Indeed if nothing else at all had happened that day (and I believed a great deal had) a whole class had given careful and respectful attention to a work of art from the past. They had seen it in a framework – how was it made? – they had studied it with care; next time they visited a museum, they would be able to look and think, and see people as well as gold, see the need to look with care.

I mentioned in the last sequence the boy who was so lost in his work that he used his most natural language, and that leads me to the final gift of drama to the history teacher. It is sometimes difficult to talk of pleasure and comfort in teaching, partly because of a puritan ethic that makes one feel education should be hard work, and partly from observance of the staff-room convention that it's a battlefield out there. Certainly many teachers find it strange and somehow wrong when I talk of my pleasure in teaching, and my need for comfortable relationships.

I must try to illustrate what I mean. Recently I was set a particularly difficult task in teaching involving appreciation of an abstract work of art. I had to move gently towards a position in which the children could be triggered to talk about the picture in a positive way, unhampered by inhibitions. Towards the end of the lesson, as we sat together on the floor of the gallery (surrounded by a crowd of official, and, increasingly, unofficial observers) the children began to talk in a reflective, unforced way, with no hands up, throwing in ideas as they came, not bothering to notice that there was any conflict in their views, just gently talking.

That gave me great pleasure for two reasons: despite the difficult circumstances, we were managing to relate happily outside the conventional structures school so often imposes, and there was both sharing and equality in that relationship; but in addition it was that context, and that alone, which would allow me to reach my objective – the children could only make personal appreciations of the picture if the situation lacked force, and the observations they made were powerful – far better in quality (to my mind) than any comment any adult had made to me.

Thus although I may sound somewhat idealistic and soft in wanting comfortable teaching relations with children, I also have some very hard-edged educational reasons for needing them, too. It is worth making a little list of these, for although I see at once that not all teachers will want the somewhat avuncular relationship I enjoy most

121

in my teaching, I do think many teachers will see the educational values of such a style of work, and will be able to build in their preferred form of relationship to it.

Basically this kind of work depends on three things one must win from and for the children: willing participation; willingness to listen to others and see the sense of relating to what others have to say in this mutual enterprise of learning; and the understanding that one may do better if one tries, and the willingness to try.

Winning participation is a complex procedure, for it has nothing to do with forcing everyone to join in: one thing I have learned very slowly as a teacher is the importance of letting the shy and reserved watch and think – a year or so ago I allowed two girls seemingly to swim with the tide for fifteen hours of work before they suddenly entered the drama and made a magical climax for it. No, you must win trust by establishing that you are honest and reliable, you do not play tricks on children, and you do always listen seriously; you may laugh with them to hysteria, but you never never laugh at what they have to say when they are serious. Above all you must show in every way you know that they have a right to say something in this matter, and that it will be worthy of attention.

To do this is especially difficult in certain circumstances, for the conventions of the social system of the school build up the authority of the teacher, the passivity and unreliability, the immaturity of the child. When I come to a school to teach, I carry a double weight of authority, for I am Doctor Fines, the learned man, the famous man who is watched by teachers; there is an audience, and no doubt the day before the headmaster has warned them all to be on their best behaviour, OR ELSE. . . . So to them the most sensible stance is to sit back and listen, sit tight and say nuffin. Thus I have to go to somewhat absurd attempts to get rid of my authority and place the responsibility back on the learners' shoulders; often the role is the clue in all this – I have learned frequently to take roles that lower, that demean, my own status. I noticed this first when working with a group of pupils who had very little respect for their own ability on a project about old age. The key for them came when I took the role of a senile old man they had to care for. I did very annoying things, like losing my keys, and they had to search around in my pockets for them, saying 'come on, pop, they must be somewhere'. With each session their ability to contribute grew, and what I noticed with great interest (and some relief, naturally) was that as soon as I put down the stick and became the teacher again, they recognized the change of role, the change of relationship. This they tended to exaggerate for themselves, for although I had urged them to use my Christian name, at all points when they had stopped dealing with 'pop', I was then Doctor Fines, in most formal manner.

As one breaks through the conventions of normal school relations to work with children on much more equal terms, as full participants in their own learning, there is great pleasure, and great desire to do better. I recall now ruefully the days when I fought to make children obey me, and got surprisingly little pleasure from the work, and grew more and more pessimistic about the possibility of progress. Now I have stopped fighting I am always thinking about doing better, about them doing better.

To do this one must constantly praise that which is good in the children's work, so that they can see in the clearest possible way the direction of growth. The best of today must be made better tomorrow, so when someone finds some good words in a particular situation one must find time to brood on the quality of the words, note where they are doing a good job, express one's pleasure in the child's success, in the hopes that this will breed more.

For me this is the ultimate aim of all – that pupils should have pride in speech, as a part of a shared enterprise. Were one to be offered three things for a child in school – literacy, numeracy and oracy – I know where I would put my money. To think hard and be able to speak those thoughts in a willing debate is the best of all the skills. We may forget the history we learn, the dates, the names, the details, but if it has been a medium for this kind of achievement, it has earned its place in the curriculum. In my own struggle to get there as a history teacher, drama, whatever that funny name means, has served me well, and I express my gratitude with pleasure.

7 *Drama and the arts*

Julian Watson

The curriculum of any school must, of necessity, include a great deal of repetition. Young children do not understand ideas and concepts upon first experience, and one of the teacher's inevitable problems is how to present the same material a number of times without losing motivation on the part of the child. The arts can help in the varied presentation of such material. They will allow the child to experience a concept through different senses, preserving his interest whilst repeating the idea. In its simplest form this can mean that the child paints a picture, makes a model, writes a poem and acts out a role, all connected with the same area of learning. In the process he comes to a fuller understanding of the concept or idea. It is not simply that an experience triggers off the learning mechanism in that particular child, but that he gains a fuller understanding of the topic by his engagement with a variety of media.

This argument has resulted in projects, topics, themes and other forms of integrated studies being included in the curriculum. However there is a danger that such a well-rehearsed argument loses some of its important subtleties. Engagement with a variety of media means much more than the use of a number of different materials. The materials may be the most visible part of the process, but if they are to contribute to a deeper understanding then they must be the external signals for variety of thought.

It is quite possible for a child to produce written work, drawings and models without really changing his mode of thinking. In a project on transport he may describe different forms of vehicle, draw and paint them and make magnificent models of railway engines and the like. Yet all these media may require only one particular way of looking at the world, a way that requires an easy facility with words and a readiness to accept the experience of others. The type of intuitive thinking required by drama improvisation, the sort of thinking needed for a detailed line drawing, the appreciation of a problem in terms of plane and mass, none of these may have been attempted. The project on transport is incomplete without an experience of how planning decisions are made, of the effect on a community of a nearby motorway, of the worries of a young mother living near to a busy road, of the near-panic of a member of the planning department faced with a hostile public meeting, of the sense of loss experienced by older members of the community moved into new dwellings. All these forms of thinking will not only be an aesthetic experience in their own right, but will also deepen the understanding of the original concept, transport. It is sometimes argued that the arts are frills and luxuries in our schools. If they are contributing to the mainstream of a child's understanding they can no longer be dismissed in this way. The arts will form a bridge between the knowledge and ourselves. They can help us to make information part of ourselves.

That process of taking factual information and making it personal and thus meaningful to ourselves cannot take place without some structure or plan upon which we can hang the bits of information. There needs to be a narrative or story element running through our understanding, so that the knowledge is organized and ordered into a form we can make our own. This is a process which is particularly lacking in the area of project or topic work, as it is often called. Children are sometimes kept very busy collecting factual information and recording it, often in very lively and interesting ways, without ever making sense of the material . . . without asking why something is happening or what the consequences will be. I was recently talking to a group of bright 10- and 11-year-olds engaged in the study of the City of Chester. They had visited the town, filled in lots of worksheets, talked about their work and were then engaged upon interesting descriptive writing and illustrations of the city walls. I asked them why a city such as Chester would build such walls, why we no longer build walls around cities – questions they had not previously given any thought. With a little encouragement they were soon able to tell me, but the danger is that knowledge is seen as collection of data and not the use of that data to draw conclusions. I suspect if they had been given the opportunity to role-play the citizens of Chester at some moment of stress in their history they would know full well why the city has walls!

125

The arts will provide the personal context, which makes facts meaningful, efficiently and succinctly. Particularly perhaps in a historical context it will enable the child to relate his learning to his own experience. To study the Saxons and the Normans is one thing, to see it through the eyes of the young boy in Geoffrey Trease's novel, *Bows against the Barons*, is another. The cognitive learning can still be there – the boy lives in a Saxon Lord's household, is banished to live in the forest of Sherwood, is taken on as an apprentice in Nottingham by one of the guild craftsmen, becomes part of the revolt of the peasants, and so on. A child involved in telling this story has a framework upon which to hang his knowledge. In my school we used the novel as the basis for a maze, through which visitors had to find their way. The maze was structured so that you first passed through the small Saxon village – a guidebook, slides and models showed you the layout of the village, then rapidly progressed to the forest of Sherwood where you were relieved of your loose change by Robin himself, before being shown the road to Nottingham. In the city you were pestered by pedlars, arrested by Norman soldiers, taken to the castle and told off by the Sheriff, himself, before being thrown into dungeons, from which you escaped with the help of the Saxon 'underground' movement who made you swear an oath of secrecy before releasing you out of the fire door and on to the playing fields! Throughout the maze, decisions had had to be made, properties and costumes produced and factual work displayed. The two classrooms and a cloakroom area required were back in commission as teaching spaces with only a total lapse of four days. The learning which had gone on seemed worth the sacrifice.

Such ideas as the maze require careful planning and organization. This maze was worked upon by three separate classes, each having taken a section of the work as their focus. In this case there was little interaction between classes until the whole project was put together near the end of term, in other cases classes have worked much more as a team. In either situation forward planning is most necessary with a great deal of structure and care built into the learning experience by the staff. Certainly it is possible to disguise the amount of structure, so that children feel that they are on a genuine voyage of discovery, but it is not practical or effective to think in terms of learning alongside the child. Teachers may learn a great deal by working in this way, but they are not learning the same things that the children are learning.

In my experience planning takes place on three different levels. First, there needs to be some awareness of overall aims. In the project described above our real concern was with language. We felt that the children were limited in the number and type of registers they were able to employ. The project, therefore, deliberately asked the children to write descriptively, imaginatively, in role, at length and concisely, in both prose and poetry, and so on. That seemed to be our prime objective. Then there was another level at which the historical work was considered, the actual content prepared, to see that this was useful and interesting. Deliberately unusual aspects of the period were brought to the fore by the quality of the novel we used. Finally in terms of planning there was the outcome – the maze itself. Although the maze changed as it was erected, we nevertheless had a fairly clear vision of what we might achieve, with rough plans on paper and an awareness of resources, for example, the old stage cloth painted with a stone-wall effect, the ten ex-RAF parachutes bought and dyed to the right colour, the possibility of borrowing extra slide-projectors from the Teachers Centre. All this had to be considered in the planning, which makes it all sound rather laborious and slow. It did not feel that way, and was mostly very informal.

Through this sort of work I have become convinced of the importance of an 'outcome' for the children. If they feel they are working towards an end-product which will be of a high standard and clearly of use, then they care much more about their work. If the work is put in a folder or exercise book, perhaps shown to parents at the end of the year, and that is all, then they may quickly lose interest in the quality if not the quantity of their work. Clearly it is not necessary to produce the spectacular each time, but it is important that the children's work is constantly valued. Many schools include work from the children in weekly assemblies, where the best of the work is shared with the rest of the school community. In this way the 'ground-rules' for the school are quickly established and high standards encouraged in a positive way. Other outcomes might consist of: a duplicated booklet of poems which can be sold to parents, a slide/tape production of pictures, words and music put together by the children. (A modern slide/tape pulse unit is quite simple enough to be operated by children.) Also to be encouraged is the production of large booklets of work, factual or imaginative, usually the result of the work of a group of children who co-operate to produce the booklet and feel a certain responsibility as a result. In each case it is hoped that the individual or group feels a responsibility, feels the pressure of a deadline, understands that if his/her work is not up to scratch then others are affected.

If the children are to bear a certain responsibility for their learning it is beholden upon the teacher to organize resources and equipment so that they may work effectively. We always seem to begin with books, the lifeblood of projects like this, and the collection of suitable material needs to begin some time before the project commences. My own local authority has an excellent children's library, housed in the same building as the central library, which offers a 'Project Box' service, as I believe do many libraries throughout the country. Given some notes on the project our children's librarian will use her knowledge and skill to assemble books on the chosen area. These are retained in school for a term, supplementing the school's own resources considerably.

Books within the school library again need organization, and young children do find a library very daunting. They can only be led towards an understanding of the mysteries of Dewey. For this reason our library has been colour-coded parallel with the Dewey classification, and further, the books on a particular project will be displayed separately. Each book is turned to show its face rather than spine, and a small card placed under it, detailing author and title. Children know that books may be borrowed for the day, but must be returned at home-time. The cards provide a check of what is missing.

So books are the beginning, but rapidly we turn to illustrations, slides, films and, wherever possible, real objects. The resource I value most highly however, is an 'expert'. Someone with a passion for a subject will communicate at least some of his enthusiasm to the children, even if totally unused to talking in school. Contacts from friends of staff or small references in local papers have led us to meet local historians, musicians who make their own period instruments, the deputy-manager of a newsagents shop who has his own Indian tepee and a museum of artifacts in his bedroom, local teachers who have established a 'Dark Ages' society where long nights are spent making chain-mail in the correct, original manner which is then donned for battles held on local heathlands. Perhaps most valuable of all was the afternoon tea we held in school, where the children made cakes and sandwiches and sent invitations to the older folk who had lived in the area since childhood. A tape-recorder on each table and some carefully selected questions led to a wonderful afternoon where history was appreciated in a whole new light. The old folks talked of 'being in service', of spending hours 'dollying the tub' of making aprons from sugar bags and collecting their wages in pence at the end of the week. No textbook or other resource could have been so effective, nor provided such an enthusiastic audience later in the term when the children presented their story of the local area as a documentary drama.

The organization and planning of such work needs to begin perhaps a term in advance so that full advantage can be taken of experts, resources and educational visits. Our projects have so far spanned one school term, with a concentrated period of stimulation early on. Novels and, more particularly, poems on the theme are read to the children and usually a large model or other spectacular art project begun, to fire the children with interest and enthusiasm. If possible a display, set up by staff during the holiday, greets children as they enter school for a new term, or perhaps shows them the different sections of the project so that they can see how their work will relate to that of others. Indeed the division of the work into sections is a very important part of our planning. Each teacher will be responsible for the work or story and they will sub-divide the work for their groups. Much discussion will also have been entered into concerning the initial stimulus, perhaps a 'master lesson' from more than one member of staff, or a particularly vivid film we have been able to borrow. The emphasis is upon *input*, with little writing or other output expected from the children at these early stages. We hope to raise the interest level and pose some questions, and drama is of course an ideal vehicle for this.

Initially the drama work will have two parallel strands, the first concerns skills, and here I lean heavily on the work of Viola Spolin (1973), the second uses those skills to explore the particular problems thrown up by the project in hand.

These two strands would be apparent in each session, but the balance will shift from one to the other as the situation demands. I find great security in Spolin's structure of What/Where/Who and know I can always return to it when the exploration either runs out of steam, or poses a problem for which the children have no answer. I am sure all teachers of drama need a similar survival kit which is also useful in its own right.

Early drama sessions with inexperienced children will, therefore, spend considerable time on such skills as keeping one's attention on the job in hand, refusing to be distracted by anything, and by

129

introducing the children to the idea of conscious belief in an unreal situation – the suspension of disbelief, as it has been called elsewhere. As in the other arts however, there is little fun or profit in practising a skill which one rarely uses, and so even in very early sessions the children will be placed in an improvisational situation, usually in small groups, and asked to explore that situation for a few minutes. It seems most helpful to break into their playing at frequent intervals, discussing, making some point then asking them to continue, rather than expecting them to sustain their work for very long. The work will usually be very rough in nature and full of anachronisms and mistakes of detail. No matter if the children do sit watching television in their Saxon hovel! That matters less than their commitment to the task, and it will almost certainly be picked up by others in the group when discussion takes over from action.

Towards the end of each session I try to spend time collecting the ideas which have come up in our time together, and often ask the children to write down lists of things they need to find out, things it would be helpful to have next time, books they need to consult. This does seem to prove one of the best ways of bringing about real research in the children. If, for their improvisation next time, they need to know how the land was ploughed or what jobs were most important in the village, they will certainly find out!

Similar lists will be used throughout the project, asking children for the properties they need or the costumes which would help either action or atmosphere. And all the time the children are being taught deliberately and carefully the skills they need to employ. This task is made so much easier when the children can see the immediate need for that skill, and the younger the child the more immediate the demonstration needs to be. Nevertheless there is a real need for input of skills, and we should not be ashamed of that. A few years ago such work would have been frowned upon, as we were all swept along in a wave of spontaneity and creativity. Let us hope that those two vital ingredients have now assumed their rightful place in the order of things. The arts are above all a disciplined business, and children happily accept that discipline provided that the reason for its existence is clear to them.

Children are, therefore, given lots of poems to read, or hear many read before they are asked to write themselves. They collect interesting words from a dictionary and a thesaurus, they list useful images or ideas, a small group may contribute a line each to a group poem, and certainly individual poems will be discussed and rewritten several times before they are completed. Similarly the pleasant sounding phrase which a group of children discover on their pentatonic percussion instruments, will be reworked and adapted with suggestions from several sources. Movement skills will be taught and practised thoroughly in movement sessions. The children will not gain an insight into the nature of dance if their understanding of, for example, weight and time is incomplete. Without the skill, the feeling is never created. It remains empty physical movement.

Individual skills such as these are essential, and need deliberate teaching, need teaching to the point where they become meaningful to the child. Clearly there are always problems when dealing with feeling and the emotions in the school context, but without confronting that problem little progress will be made. I find it necessary to avoid direct description of the feeling aspect, rather working towards it by manipulation of the material and group situation. Children spend a great deal of time working individually these days, perhaps too much time. The treadmill of one workcard followed by another can be a lonely and dispiriting business. Both movement and drama can do a great deal to balance this experience, giving children the opportunity to practise the flexible, social interaction which makes up a vital part of the adult world.

In most classes there will be a fair proportion of children capable of leading a group, giving out the ideas, and generally moving the others along, either in movement or in drama. A skill which is much less common is the ability to accept the suggestions of others and build upon those ideas. Several theatre games are available which assist with the consideration of this skill, but it is not something which can be quickly developed. Once it appears there seems to be a great increase in the potential output. A new momentum is created, as one idea sparks off another. Such work is clearly visible in movement, particularly in the early improvisatory moments, as a group feels its way towards the answering of a task. It can also be observed in drama where an idea is teased and extended, rather than quickly explored and then replaced with another. When children are able to work in this manner it becomes quite clear how the concept of discipline can be learnt through work in the arts. It does take great self-control to work *with* the idea of another, rather than replacing it with one of your own. I have seen many adult groups fail at such a challenge. This aspect of working in groups seems to me to be so important that I would like to illustrate it further.

131

Clearly young children are not miniature adults, they do think differently and behave differently at each stage of development. Certainly very young children find it impossible to work with any real co-operation with more than one other person. Nevertheless this sensitivity towards the needs of others in the working situation seems to me to be so important that I would encourage its experience from a very early age. Whenever possible a group of children are made to feel responsible to each other and to the task. It is their job to complete the task, their group responsibility. They must help each other in the amassing of material, in the organization of that material, in the decisions as to what needs copying out, what needs illustrating. They must put the material together into some coherent form, perhaps making a large book with an interesting cover which is designed to make others pick it up and look at it. Upon opening the book a contents page will be needed to show what the book contains, and the material will be divided logically into sensibly ordered sections. Books of factual material, books of poems, books which tell an imaginative story, can all be treated in this way, although of course a member of staff will do all they can to assist and advise. More realistically it is the role of that member of staff to see that the task really is completed, without the danger of any major failures. They need to be there when decisions are made, to see that tasks are realistic and that individuals are capable of the work asked of them. They will need to steer the discussions and feed in the information, but hopefully the children will feel the responsibility is theirs.

Such written work is often closely linked to the material being considered in drama improvisations. For instance, in the work we did on the North American Indian culture, children were given the task of reflecting the different types of Indian both in written terms and as part of the documentary. They had to investigate life-styles and cultures and select interesting information, which would either be best communicated by the written word or dramatic performance. This work was part of a larger project in which two classes of children were involved. One class looked at the North American Indian culture, the other at the reasons for settlers leaving Europe and journeying to the New World. Groups of children worked on the different tribes, as described above, while others looked at the explorers and then settlers – who they were and where they came from. We were able to obtain a passenger list from the *Mayflower* and trace some of the names there back to villages in England. This allowed much role-play as a result of research, with scenes of religious persecution, scenes on board the early sailing ships, scenes of the Pilgrim Fathers making contact with Indian tribes and many more. In almost every case children were initially asked to improvise, but then told to continue their role-play on paper. Writing in role is something which seems to prove very fruitful, both from the point of view of later improvisations and as a vehicle for an understanding of register and 'audience'.

James Britten has written and lectured extensively about the concept of audience affecting children's writing. It is a complex idea and one which continues to exercise my thoughts. Nevertheless I have found the process of writing in role to be a most useful way of showing that *how* we write is dependent upon *to whom* we write. Very few of the children I encounter have this concept clear in their conscious thinking. Certainly they have different registers, which they employ in classroom or playground, but they are not aware that adults, too, adjust their speech, behaviour and writing, depending on the circumstances or audience. Links can very quickly be drawn between the children writing 'as if' they are a particular individual and the variety of roles they themselves play in the course of a normal day. Such writing also constantly keeps in the child's mind that he is writing for a reason, not just for the teacher to mark. This sense of communication is something I believe to be of great importance and which I encourage in positive ways. So, children are asked to write letters in a variety of roles: as an apprentice in Nottingham who is sending his first letter home to his nervous mother; a page-boy in Nottingham Castle comparing conditions of work with another boy in a different castle; a settler who has just landed in America and tries to describe it all to relations at home; a local politician who is writing his notes for his speech tonight, or a railwayman writing a song he will sing in the pub tonight which tells of his boss's mistakes.

The same concern for communication is probably one of the reasons why many of our projects end in a documentary drama or similar presentation. Nothing seems more beneficial to learning than the act of explaining the content to someone else, as anyone who teaches must have noticed. Hopefully the children involved in a documentary feel that they have some knowledge to share, that they know things that their parents or the other children do not, and the presentation is designed to share that information – to tell the story of their research. What they have learned has to be communicated to others, and in the process much more is learned.

133

Such an attitude gives added weight to research, and makes many of the tasks much more real. Children attempting to construct a full-size model of a tepee see the task not as model-making or set design, but as an attempt to show others the excitement of learning they have personally experienced. Poems written to illustrate the working conditions of nailmakers in the last century are not merely an exercise with words, but a way of sharing the information and concern.

We work towards a presentation over perhaps a term, and initial drama improvisations are extended and reworked as the knowledge of the children increases. As more information becomes available so the drama can become better informed, the gossip more relevant, the argument better founded.

Again the research and factual matter is being *put to use*, not merely copied out. A further advantage of this approach is that much of the material is brought out into the open and, therefore, misconceptions are much easier to deal with. Children learn so naturally and easily from their peers and often a disagreement over the relative importance of an issue, or a factual detail, can be a significant period of learning for the whole group.

As we progress through the term the number of new ideas begins to diminish and attention swings towards the need for precision and repetition. The movement sequence is not complete until it can be repeated exactly, the music will need practice and perhaps the size of the playing group will extend, poems will need editing and copying out. I have already mentioned the taking of school assembly by the children, and this does give an opportunity for work to be displayed and its effect considered. Not that we consciously use assembly as a trial ground, but we do find that individual sections of the story are of great interest to the children concerned and they may well wish to share this with the rest of the school. In our last project that centred on Elizabeth I and her Royal Progress to Kenilworth Castle, we had assemblies that considered the poor of London at that period, the miseries of death and disease, the life of William Shakespeare, the lavish entertainments laid on for Her Majesty, and the small village celebrations along the route. Soon after the mid point in the term we begin to think about how such sections can be brought together.

Our initial planning did consider the nature of the presentation, and rough ideas are often drafted, but once all the factual material has been fully explored by the children there are inevitably changes in our original thinking. Some sections which appeared exciting have not been so successful with the children, other sections have not been covered because of the pressure of time, whole new sections have emerged as worthy of inclusion. What we now must seek is a documentary which tells our story and has dramatic interest as well as factual accuracy.

The project will now be within two or three weeks of its conclusion and we are very aware that the freshness and excitement of the children's work can rapidly diminish if too many rehearsals are attempted. Much more work is, therefore, done with staff acting as links, and with isolated groups of children, thus saving the excitement of starting to see the whole theme emerge until a little later. Very often the linking of individual scenes can be arranged by the children reading their poems or other written work. We use a simple microphone system so that even the smallest of voices can be heard, regardless of what is going on 'on stage'. Our stage consists of a large square of plain carpet, set in the middle of the school hall. We always work in-the-round, finding that this form of presentation requires the least change in the children's work. They are used to working in the body of the hall and they continue to do so. The fact that we begin to think about an audience sitting round the edge of the hall seems to affect them very little.

In my own teacher-training much was made of the difference between curriculum drama and the act of showing. It was suggested that there is a great difference between child drama and theatre. I would not question that statement some fifteen years of experience later, but I would wonder about its importance. Certainly the children I teach seem to find the transition from something we explore together to something we share with others, much easier than I was led to expect. As we approach the final week before our presentation I do find myself talking of clarity of speech, of stillness being as important as movement, of the necessity for speed and silence during changes of scene, but these theatrical matters are shared with the children and they seem to make them their own. If we are concerned with telling a story (and is theatre ever concerned with anything else?), then we need to be efficient in the telling. If we are concerned with the education of the whole child, then the same criteria apply, for a clear storyline will mean efficent learning. And as long as we remain within an 'ensemble' approach to presentation, then it seems that education and theatre can happily co-exist.

The use of theatrical devices at this stage of the project seem further

135

justified by the deepening of experience which those involved in the story-telling can receive. During the North American Indian documentary we portrayed the birth of Tecumsah, who grew up to be a great chief of the Shawnee tribe. As he was born a meteor passed over the camp, and I fully remember the atmosphere on the first occasions when we played that scene in full costume, lit by little red torches as firelight, and with just the right sound effect which a member of staff had found the previous day. Those children felt something of lasting worth, and will still happily describe every detail.

Simple theatrical effects are employed where possible. We have the use of eight lights and a portable dimmer board, which does more than anything to aid the creation of atmosphere. Large models are often made with wire-netting and pasted paper, but are made to appear as authentic as possible. Smaller items use the real materials if we can obtain them. If an Apache loom is required then it is constructed so that it will work, and much learnt about weaving in the process. Costumes again are as authentic as possible, and children are heavily involved in the making of them.

Considerable use is made of the children's own music in the performance, again sometimes forming a useful linking mechanism between sections. New words are written to old tunes, or words and music may both be created. We have a large selection of tuned and untuned percussion instruments and the children are able to play these at playtimes as well as in more formal situations.

Some presentations require more in the way of theatrical effects than others. Occasionally we have needed lighting effects which have been beyond our little board, and have therefore used slide-projectors with homemade ink slides in them – an excellent swamp for Grendal to live in! Often the overhead projector is used as a light source. It is easy to create colour and shape using simply constructed templates. Children thought of the idea of using the overhead projector as a puppet theatre, mounting little figures on acetate and moving them over a background which could scroll up or down most effectively. Constantly we are looking for the most interesting way of making a particular point. We draw inspiration from professional theatre, particularly the few who operate in-the-round, and our style of playing does seem to have links with street theatre, or early mystery plays. These forms of theatre have a strong storyline to put over and both often use narration as a device to hold the whole performance together.

As a head teacher who believes in and tries to foster the arts I have always felt it important to keep parents very well-informed as to what is going on in school. It would be quite possible for a parent to see their children involved in one of these projects for perhaps a third of each week and for them to questions the value in terms of the necessary basic skills. I see it as part of my job to do the explaining, showing them the structured-skills teaching that is still going on and helping them to recognize how basic skills are being both developed and made use of in the project work. Parents seem to appreciate the approach of learning through doing a job of work and support us enthusiastically, particularly when it has been possible to involve them from an early stage in the project. I have also encouraged parents into our weekly assembly, the one taken by the children. They have a cup of tea afterwards and enjoy the chance to chat. Further I have made several short films which have been projected prior to the performance of documentaries or the like, showing all the work which has gone into the project. They are thus aware of all that has led up to the end-product which they see before them.

If the arts can significantly deepen the understanding of academic concepts, making factual material more memorable whilst also giving experience of the aesthetic mode, then this is an important factor in curriculum planning. Further, children seem to respond to the responsibility and excitement of documentary outcomes. Reason is given to their investigations and they are encouraged to draw conclusions and appreciate consequences. Drama in particular seems to provide the human context which links learning with the child's own experience. Taken together, these factors do seem to suggest that drama and the arts in general should be seen not as an unimportant luxury, but as a formidable teaching vehicle.

PART THREE

Wider Contexts

8 *Pupil assessment and the public examination system*

Barbara Lanning

Until comparatively recent years the only drama examinations available to schools were those which stressed individual performance skills. Most of these are still in existence. Some, such as those administered by The English Speaking Board, concentrate on the ability to speak with confidence, clarity and fluency in public. Others, for example the Guildhall and LAMDA series are intended to promote acting skills, though ironically many of the full-time drama colleges training students for the profession tend to discount such qualifications when selecting applicants for admission. It is good to see that at last a dialogue has been established to see how this position may be improved. Schools offering pupils the opportunity to sit such exams were, and still are, a minority, albeit an enthusiastic one, which remains numerically constant. It used to be common to hear the majority of drama teachers voice grave reservations about examinations in their subject. School drama was not designed to encourage children to become professional actors, in fact it is usually in the pupil's best interests for it to be positively discouraging. Moreover drama ought to be fostering group- rather than individual-work. But the most common criticism of all was that the true value of drama was not quantifiable in numerical terms.

The number of school pupils entered for drama examinations has risen radically since the introduction in the late 1960s of the Certificate of Secondary Education, or, to give it its popular name, CSE. Contrary to popular opinion this series of examinations was not conceived as a soft option to the well-established General Certificate of Education with its Ordinary and Advanced levels testing the traditional academic subjects. The original intention was that CSE exams should

141

meet the needs of pupils with practical skills, such as tailoring or seamanship, whose only previous opportunity to gain a qualification had been a myriad of vocational trade or craft tests, none of which was designed for school consumption.

The emphasis on practical tests, to be carried out within the candidate's own school, meant that the boards which were set up to administer the CSE differed from their GCE counterparts in one important respect. Whereas any number of examination scripts can be sent any distance through the post, there is a limit to the amount of travelling which the assessor of practical tests can undertake. It must be remembered that all examining and moderating appointments are part-time ones, and that many of those who carry them out have full-time posts as well. It is, therefore, possible for only very few schools to reject the syllabus of their nearest CSE Board in favour of another.

Drama quickly became a well-established CSE subject and it may well be that its success was in part responsible for the appearance of an O-, O/A- and, eventually, A-level in drama in recent years. If these exams continue to attract candidates at their present rate it would suggest that drama has a good chance of being on offer when the CSE and O-levels are amalgamated in a few years' time to form the new 16-plus exam which will replace them.

Popularity alone is of course no justification for change of any kind. There are still teachers who sincerely doubt the validity of drama examinations and view their colleagues' enthusiasm to participate in the system as the rush of lemmings to the sea. It cannot be denied that of late some teachers have seen the adoption of a CSE or O-level programme as a means of securing their subject's place in a school curriculum at a time when stringent economic cuts are being made. The exams themselves, however, were conceived and inaugurated before such pragmatic considerations became relevant, and though a number of reasons have been given for their inception many see their presence as the logical conclusion to the growing awareness among drama teachers of the urgent need to articulate aims and objectives with clarity and precision. Others see drama as comparable to music, art and creative writing, which have all been assessed by a centralized system for many years.

When drama first became a common subject in the school curriculum its advocates were sometimes guilty of making very over-inflated claims for it, the chief one being that it alone provided an outlet for personal creativity which engendered great emotional satisfaction. This aspect of drama was perhaps over-emphasized by those teachers who did not encounter it until they themselves were adults. Upon serious reflection it is soon aparent that not all individuals realize their creative potential in the same way. It is now commonly recognized that not only the creative arts but any serious discipline may engender a revelation of self with the keenness of a major emotional experience. Drama teachers who claimed that it was neither possible nor desirable that this experience should be assessed in quantifiable terms were right, but they were ignoring the fact that drama had other attributes which were worthwhile for all students, whether they felt an emotional release in drama or not, and that it was not only possible but positively beneficial to submit some of these to assessment.

A teacher working regularly with the same group of pupils does not merely try to provide them with a fulfilling and enjoyable experience; as time progresses material and methods will be selected which will meet the various needs which the teacher has identified. Not all children have the same ability to concentrate, to convey ideas with fluency or to work creatively with others. The teacher is constantly assessing each individual's particular attributes as weak, average or good; when even finer distinctions are made personal assessment is falling into the same five divisions as those made by the CSE exam. A public examination gives the teacher the opportunity to match personal standards against the norm for the age-group. Such adjustments by the teacher inevitably benefit the pupils and the opportunity to do so is particularly valuable in those many schools where there is only one teacher, who is consequently denied the opportunity for discussion on such matters with colleagues.

In most areas the first CSE drama exams were those known as 'Mode Three'. In these the syllabus is drawn up and examined internally in the school with an external moderator responsible for fitting these marks into the appropriate grades. A few areas inaugurated the alternative 'Mode One' system where there is a common syllabus and an external examiner to assess the majority of the work. For the sake of clarity I am using the term Mode One to cover instances of 'Mode Two' as well, since the two systems operate identically at school level, the only difference between them being the way the subject panel which controls the exam is constituted.

Mode One syllabuses are drawn up by a panel elected by and from

143

the drama teachers in the area covered by each particular board. Such panels have power to co-opt non-voting members. These include those with specialist knowledge, such as a local drama Adviser, and those who can give advice on the way the exam will be received by prospective employers. All decisions made by such a panel are subject to approval by the board's central Examinations Committee which may already have laid down certain general guidelines for all the syllabuses under its control. For example, the maximum and minimum percentage of marks which may be awarded to any kind of practical work.

It is essential that when a syllabus has been approved guidelines for those who will mark it are drawn up summarizing the standard required for each grade. In order that marking is consistent throughout the exam it is customary to call all examiners and moderators to a standardizing meeting just before they begin. Having seen work similar to that which will be presented for the exam, each individual is asked to mark it. It is then possible to identify any one whose marks do not accord with the rest and ensure that such an individual adjusts his or her standards. There is generally, however, a reassuring measure of agreement. One examinations board requires all teachers following a Mode Three system to attend a similar meeting every year.

Teachers are divided on the relative merits of the Mode One and Mode Three systems. There are obvious advantages in being the captain of one's own fate and marking one's own pupils' work, especially in schools which have devised a syllabus to incorporate their own particular specializations. In some schools, for instance, several other departments participate with great enthusiasm. Whereas a syllabus designed for general use could not make it compulsory for every candidate to research and make an historical costume or demonstrate a lighting plan in practice, this is possible under a Mode Three syllabus.

Other teachers argue that they feel unable to make totally objective judgements on work with which they have been closely involved; it is very difficult to reward a candidate who has attained a high standard in practical presentation in fair measure, if one is aware of how often that individual has stayed away from rehearsals. It is also a great temptation to grade the hard-working and low achiever at a higher level than that actually attained. Drama exams must measure attainment and not effort if they are to be accepted as a serious method of assessment. It is perhaps significant that at least one region which began by offering only a Mode Three system adopted a Mode One alternative at the request of the teachers in that area.

It is to be hoped that in a few years' time every drama teacher will have the option of adopting either a Mode One or a Mode Three system and the choice will entirely depend upon the needs of the pupils in each particular school. There is, however, at least one regional examining board which has such grave reservations over the true objectivity of assessing practical drama work, that it is not as yet prepared to allow a Mode One proposal to go forward. For reasons given above the schools in this area cannot remuster *en bloc* to follow the Mode One syllabus of another board. There is also fear in some quarters that the advent of the new 16-plus exam may abolish the Mode Three system of assessment altogether, especially if employers continue to show a preference for Mode One qualifications over Mode Three.

It was probably an over-anxious wish to demonstrate to colleagues in other subjects that drama possessed its own rigorous academic standards that was reponsible for the attempt by the first syllabuses to cover too many aspects. This is a criticism which can still be applied in specific instances. Most teachers quickly realized that, just as English literature examines candidates on a very limited number of books, so drama should select and specialize on a limited number of areas. It was also obvious that there were two diverse approaches as to the kind of study and, as a result, the terms drama and theatre arts (or occasionally theatre studies) came into use. In order to define the differences between the two the Schools Council set up a working party and the bulletin which it published, *Examinations In Drama* (1974), has since provided helpful guidelines for those wishing to draft a new syllabus. It is perhaps unnecessary to reiterate the definitions laid out by this working party in full, but to summarize their conclusions: theatre arts concern all the skills involved in the presentation of a play to an audience; drama often takes place without spectators present and seeks to develop those qualities which are of value when all members of a group are involved in spontaneous improvisation. There is, of course, an area which is common to both drama and theatre arts. This, and the fundamental differences between them, is probably best demonstrated if the individual components of each exam are analysed, and, since it was first in the field and is by far the most common, it is logical to begin with CSE.

In the assessment of both drama and theatre arts there is strong emphasis on participation in practical tests, though at least one board does not permit this work to carry more than 50 per cent of the marks. As most pupils study the course over two years, it is also common for there to be two practical tests, one at the end of the year in which pupils attain the age of 15 and one at the end of the second term or the beginning of the third term in the following year. For theatre arts the first presentation is often a play or series of scenes which are rehearsed versions of improvisational work in class. The second theatre arts presentation is normally scripted work. A few teachers prefer to reverse this order and begin with the scripted work but most consider that pupils need the confidence of conveying their own ideas in their own words before they are ready to interpret and perform the printed word. There is enormous variation in the conditions of performance at each level. Some teachers feel that both tests should be full productions with lighting, costume, make-up and scenery the responsibility of the candidates, whereas others believe that this imposes too great a burden on the first year where the work should emphasize the ability to adopt and sustain a role and convey ideas and emotions with appropriate language and movement. Most teachers agree that every candidate should participate as an actor in the first production, but should be allowed to offer an alternative skill, such as responsibility for lighting or sound effects in the second practical test. Whatever the choice it is absolutely essential that the contribution of each individual is identifiable within the corporate effort and it is normal for the moderator/examiner to have access to the notes made by anyone offering a 'backstage' skill. It is not advisable to allow candidates to be marked on their contribution to a number of such areas since this cannot be compared with the effort made in one particular part of the work.

One of the greatest difficulties facing those teaching a theatre arts syllabus is the limited choice of worthwhile scripted plays suitable for this age-range. There are instances of excellent performances of Shakespeare but this is not the normal standard of attainment which is expected at this level. It is also questionable whether a candidate ought to be asked to participate in a production which lasts for longer than two hours, and, in recent years, certain syllabuses have laid down strict time limits for this section of the work. In many instances the problem of selecting suitable material which gives each participant an equal opportunity to show his or her abilities has been overcome by presenting a series of scenes, generally based on some common theme such as the relationship between parents and children. There appears to be far less concern over the choice of scripts available to single sex schools. Possibly it is a measure of the way our society is changing that it is almost as common to see boys choose to play serious female roles as the reverse, though few teachers would feel that this is something that can be insisted upon. Some of the most successful and polished productions have been of musical plays. This naturally depends upon the willingness of the music department to participate and it is a matter of great astonishment that there appear to be hardly any CSE syllabuses which combine theatre arts or drama with music. Some teachers overcome the difficulty of finding a suitable script by writing their own. From *Ralph Roister Doister* to *Joseph and the Amazing Technicolor Dreamcoat* our national culture has been enriched by plays written initially for schools, but not all aspiring teacher/playwrights attain such heights. Before permitting such entries a board ought to ask itself if it is proper to expose candidates to the risk of having to perform poorly-written material.

The presentation of a miscellany also gives provision for individual items to be presented. Some Mode Three syllabuses actually insist that every candidate should perform a solo piece and allocate a separate range of marks for it. The chief criticisms of such work are that this is not a corporate activity and does not encourage co-operation within a group; it is also a method of testing which makes the low achievers very nervous and in consequence they do less well than when they are participating in a combined effort.

Another problem which became apparent when the theatre arts exams were first put into practice was that of the audience. It is probably unfair to the majority of candidates to permit either practical test to take place in front of a great number of spectators. Other pupils can be over-boisterous or inattentive and cause candidates to lose concentration. Parents, too, are not always sensitive to the effect which their presence can create, and there have been instances where a performance has been frequently interrupted with the flashlight of a proud father's camera. On the other hand the single figure of the moderator/examiner in the auditorium can be equally off-putting, especially if the style of the play demands reaction from those watching. Participants in melodrama often gain encouragement and confidence from the boos and cheers they receive. Possibly the best audience is the one selected by the teacher responsible for the group, but a syllabus ought to contain some regulation which enables that

147

teacher to tactfully refuse entry to other classes if the exam takes place in school time. A drama or theatre arts exam should never be regarded by colleagues as a means of obtaining a free period. There is after all no reason why a rehearsed production may not be presented on another occasion when any number of parents and friends may come.

There are two forms in which the first practical test for drama usually appears. In some cases the candidates present work which has arisen in class as spontaneous improvisation and which has been polished to improve its shape and coherence. Although this is similar to the first practical test in theatre arts, it is customary to assess not only the standard of the final performance but also each individual's contribution to the preparation. Teachers are asked to keep a written record of those who contributed the ideas and those who were responsible for forming them into dramatic shape. These profiles are then presented to the moderator/examiner at the exam. This method is well suited to Mode Three work but is far less satisfactory in a Mode One where the visiting examiner is responsible for all the marking.

The other form which the first practical test often takes in CSE drama is the totally unprepared session led by the teacher, adopting his or her usual teaching approach. It is wrong to think of such sessions as lessons since the numbers have to be small enough for the examiner or moderator to identify each individual and such a session usually lasts considerably longer than a normal lesson. The most frequent criticism of this method is that it is as much a test for the teacher as for the candidates, but this is not really true. Any group, entering any kind of exam, will reflect the quality of the teaching with which they have been prepared. This is not to deny that even the most gifted teachers will find this method of assessment a difficult personal experience, but as compensation they have the knowledge that it has several unique features. It demonstrates, as no other way can, those children who can work creatively with others; who are able to take the lead or follow another's ideas as the situation requires. Such sessions frequently confront the candidates with a problem of a personal, social or political nature and encourages them to work out a realistic and human solution. It can also demand that the candidate uses different kinds of language appropriate to different situations. In all such sessions the contribution of each individual is unequivocally clear, there is no possibility that undue support from a teacher will go unnoticed and many consider this to be the form of drama most easily assessed objectively. The main disadvantage to such a session is that

148

the teacher leading it may not always be in a position to make a fair judgement, especially if he or she participates in the action, playing a role in order to further thought. This does not matter in a Mode One situation, but if it is a Mode Three then it is advisable to have a colleague present to make the initial assessment on behalf of the school.

It is hardly possible to give a typical example of a second practical test in CSE drama, though it is generally agreed that it is advisable to adopt a different form from the first one and show another aspect of the candidates' work. A school which has offered one of the two forms described above for the first practical test, may well adopt the other for its second session. The only difference would be in the level of attainment considered as average. A third alternative is to present scripted work or a mixture of this and rehearsed improvisation, though there is a general consensus of opinion that candidates offering drama should not be compelled to include scripted work. Neither is it considered necessary to present this with full theatrical accoutrements, but schools are encouraged to put the onus on the pupils to select their own theme and material. It is not considered appropriate for candidates to offer a backstage skill as an alternative to participating in the second presentation.

A number of both theatre arts and drama examinations require participants to evaluate their own and others work immediately after the end of an examination session. This is not usually as formal as a *viva voce*, indeed it is frequently a relaxed occasion on which the group meets to reflect on and define its experiences. Teachers are divided on how much each individual should be drawn out. Some go to great lengths to ensure that each candidate is asked the same number of questions; others make it clear beforehand that this is part of the exam for which marks are awarded and it is each individual's responsibility to contribute. Though the discussion relates to the work, it is not always easy to equate achievement in such a discussion with that in the practical work to which it relates and, for administrative purposes, it is best to award this part of the exam its own percentage of marks, as happens when candidates are required to participate in a more general discussion covering all aspects of the syllabus, which usually takes place at a later date.

The decision to opt for either drama or theatre arts does not mean that it is no longer necessary to articulate aims and objectives. Within both areas there is still a great deal of choice and it is vital that the

149

syllabus should define which have been selected. In recent years the practice has arisen of stating which abilities are to be tested in each part of the exam. This is particularly helpful as practical drama work is of such a different nature from written work. It also means that it is possible to emphasize one element more than another. Teachers working with deprived children sometimes wish to place more importance on the development of language than that of movement. If this is the case then the syllabus should make it clear.

There are almost no examinations in either drama or theatre arts which do not require some kind of written work to be presented at the end of the course. The first syllabuses often asked for all or part of this to take the form of a project. It was felt that this would provide the candidate with limited writing skills with the opportunity to present work in another form, for example, a tape-recorded play or interview, a model stage with a set design or a set of puppets. Many teachers have since reversed this view, not simply because time has shown that the number of academically weak children who have taken advantage of the alternative to writing are very small indeed. The amount of time needed to give adequate supervision and help to a group of candidates each working in an area of his or her own choice is seldom available to the teacher, however generously spare time is given. Moreover the number of suitable topics available to the average child is very limited. As a result a great many less-able children have simply copied text and diagrams from standard works of reference without gaining any real insight into their subject. (Allardyce Nicoll has probably gained at least a hundred CSE awards under other names.)

Others have chosen very inappropriate fields of enquiry, such as a popular film star, and have given a factual account of the subject's life and career unredeemed by any personal response to acting performances. Those who tried to study contemporary institutions have been disappointed to find their request for information rebuffed or ignored, usually because the organization concerned has been inundated with similar requests.

There have of course been some highly intelligent and well-researched pieces of work. Candidates who studied fringe performers and groups they had seen often received a great deal of help. There have been enterprising investigations into drama facilities in neighbouring schools and local theatre-in-education teams. One candidate presented a study of the National Theatre which included not only a carefully researched history but a survey of the plays then running in the repertory and a highly intelligent criticism of the current policy on choosing plays. In an appendix the reasons for the 1979 strike by backstage workers were analysed, together with an appraisal of how fairly each national newspaper had presented the issues. This is an example of work sometimes encountered at CSE level which is so far above the norm that it would probably gain a distinction at A-level.

It cannot be denied that pupils who live where professional or amateur theatre flourishes – and this usually means town or city centres – are at a great advantage in project work. Even those living in the suburbs rarely have the opportunity to make the kind of regular visit which make such studies worthwhile. But the greatest disadvantage to project work at CSE level is that it frequently results in work which is either very good or very weak. It does not sort the candidates into the five levels of attainment required and as a method of assessment it is probably better suited to more advanced examinations.

The usual alternative to a project is a course-work file which can demonstrate both the personal response to the subject and the ability to use several different kinds of language. Such a file might include a dialogue between two characters created in an improvisation, a poem stimulated by a theme explored in a session, a letter written from a particular character's point of view, and a newspaper report of an event created in lesson time. Any one of these could be accompanied by appropriate diagrams or sketches. It is neither necessary nor desirable for a candidate to submit every piece of work completed over the two years of the course. Very often the first few attempts to evaluate a drama lesson will be a mere blow by blow account of what happened, but with the right kind of help and encouragement even the weakest candidate will begin to show a personal response and analyse why a session did or did not go well.

A theatre arts file could contain any of the pieces described above but there is a strong body of opinion which considers that the candidate should also be learning how to evaluate theatrical productions and that at least half the pieces in such a file should be accounts of plays seen in performance. These need not necessarily be professional productions, they might be visits to local amateur groups or a play staged at a neighbouring school. In the account the candidate should demonstrate an ability to apply the knowledge of practical skills learned during the course to a particular performance.

There is probably more contention over the assessment of drama or theatre arts by written examination paper than any other aspect of the syllabus. Its advocates claim that it is the only way that a fair test of the candidates' response to the practical work can be made and that if it is excluded the subject will never be accepted as equal by colleagues working in the established academic disciplines. Its critics claim that a written paper does not assess the real core of the subject and, because those who express themselves most fluently in a timed paper are not necessarily those who have most to give in practical work, a written paper can distort the results. On the whole theatre arts syllabuses use the written paper far more than does drama.

Surprisingly few misgivings have been expressed in those many cases where a theatre arts syllabus requires written course work as well as an examination paper and serious thought ought to be given to the suggestion that only one of these should be included. Where both occur it becomes very difficult to decide what the timed paper ought to be testing. Mode Three can direct its questions to the practical presentations which have formed part of the course, but this is more difficult in a centralized system where the examiner may not have seen the productions referred to. All are agreed that an examination should not merely require facts to be regurgitated. Perhaps the best way to assess how well a candidate can put his or her knowledge of theatrical skills into practice is to give a short scene or passage and ask specific questions about the problems of staging, character interpretation, designing scenery, costume or lighting and choosing sound effects. Whatever its form, the written exam ought not to duplicate other sections of the assessment, and if the course-work file were removed there would be far more point to the written paper.

There is one part of almost every CSE exam which has no counterpart at higher levels. This is the percentage of marks which the teacher can award for practical work throughout the course. The proportion of marks awarded for this part of the exam is usually very low and is the one area where the marks cannot be adjusted by an outsider. Some teachers would like to see the marks for this section of the work raised to as high a level as 50 or 60 per cent because, they say, this is the only way in which the real commitment to the subject can be rewarded. Moreover the candidates are relieved of the pressure which accrues to the exam when it is concentrated into a few, short periods of time. There are a great many drawbacks to such a method, not the least being that such a high proportion of marks must be subject to a second assessor and there is no practical way in which this can be done however carefully records of individual achievement are kept. It would also make the qualification received seem more like a teacher's termly report than an exam. When the CSE and O-levels are combined to form the new 16-plus exam it is very unlikely that the weighting given to this section will be more than 10 per cent and it may disappear altogether.

Drama does suffer from the disadvantage that it is very difficult, if not impossible, to arrange a resit for candidates who are absent through illness on the day of a practical exam. Whereas an alternative maths or geography paper of comparable standard can be set, there is no way in which a single individual can demonstrate the ability to work creatively with others. Neither would it be fair to call together all such candidates from one area on a later occasion since, even for an unprepared session, a judgement on their achievements would not be comparable to one made on a group who had worked together for at least a year. As yet no satisfactory solution has been found to this problem.

At present there are far more schools entering pupils for CSE drama than theatre arts. This is not necessarily because drama is preferred; in a number of cases schools do not possess the facilities to mount a theatre arts course. Even drama departments who do not have to share the assembly hall with a hundred-and-one other activities, frequently find their subject misunderstood by colleagues. The greatest improvement which could be made to the conditions in which the practical exams are held is not an expensive investment in equipment but in provision of an area which is free from noise. Some drama studios have actually been placed next to music practice rooms on the grounds that both engender sound. Even more unenlightened is the headteacher who is willing to switch off the school Tannoy system for an English exam, but not a drama one.

The first drama exam to be introduced at a higher level than CSE was one entitled drama and theatre arts at Ordinary (Alternative) level. Such O/A exams were introduced to provide an area of study for students in sixth forms and colleges of further education who were taking less than the usual number of A-levels and who wished to broaden the basis of their studies. Although it was intended for pupils of 17 to 19 with a more general background and maturity than those preparing for O-level at 15 to 16 years, a number of schools began to offer this O/A exam as one of the choices available to pupils at O-level. Perhaps as a result of this a true O-level, entitled simply 'drama', appeared some years later, and this has just been followed by an

153

A-level in theatre studies. Though there is still only one examination board which offers exams at all three levels, some others are beginning their own pilot schemes.

The one board which has pioneered assessment of drama and theatre arts at O- and A-levels has not enjoyed the opportunity of seeing others approach the same problems, so it has not been possible to compare one method of assessment against another. It is to be hoped that these first exams will not be viewed as blueprints to be followed unthinkingly by all those who set up O- and A-level syllabuses in their wake, but other forms of measuring ability will be tried.

Though the existing O- and O/A-exams have different titles there are strong similarities in their format and, if the Schools Council (1974) guidelines are applied, both are weighted far more towards theatre arts than drama. Obviously many of the points made about CSE exams apply here also, so comment will be restricted to the structure of these exams and the main ways in which they differ from the average CSE syllabus.

Both these exams and the A-level have a practical test, though this counts for rather less than it usually does at CSE level. The O-level has one practical exam which can be any kind of dramatic work or presentation and candidates can offer a practical skill instead of acting, providing that it is integrated with the work of the group as a whole. In the single test at O/A-level the practical work can again be either acting or a relevant skill but candidates are not compelled to work as a group and may enter individual items. Unrehearsed improvisation is not permitted. A great many teachers hope that those responsible for this rule will have second thoughts. Though spontaneous drama can be superficial and trivial, the last few years have seen the growth of a very serious approach where participants have been encouraged to identify with the problems of all sorts and conditions of fellow humans and try to work out a satisfactory resolution to the clash of interests which bedevils so many relationships at all levels of life. The kind of challenge presented in this way encourages pupils to see how social, emotional and political considerations can interrelate and need to be considered when attempting to both diagnose a problem and to remedy it. This alone would justify inclusion to unrehearsed improvisation in a liberal arts course, but it should also be remembered that the skills acquired in such work are not only used increasingly by teachers, but by social and welfare workers and personnel officers, in fact all those whose responsibilities include counselling. There are, therefore, strong grounds for including it for vocational reasons as well.

The practical content of the A-level exam falls into two parts. One of them is the demonstration of an individual skill which can take any form of off- or on-stage work. Candidates who choose acting must perform two pieces which contrast in style. All candidates must also participate in a totally original presentation created by themselves, though not all members need take an acting role. Since this exam is still in its infancy it is too early to judge if the balance it has tried to maintain between group interdependence and the development of individual potential is one which will not only enrich the life of the candidate but help to prepare each individual for the difficult transition which awaits when leaving school.

Both the O- and the O/A-level syllabuses differ from CSE exams in requiring candidates to study at least two set texts, selected from a number of options. The plays chosen may not be used in the practical tests. There is no doubt that many pupils enjoy discovering how dramatic literature can give voice to universal human dilemmas, but work on texts does present a number of problems. Practical reasons mean that a play set in a drama syllabus may not appear in the board's English literature syllabus for the same year. When a candidate studies a play as drama rather than literature some knowledge of its effectiveness in performance is required. This means that though knowledge of general theatre history is not necessary, an individual's appreciation of a play must include something of the conditions under which it was first staged, not only the physical form of the theatre but relevant social and economic facts as well. This in turn makes it hard to select a list of plays which are of equal difficulty and there have been some lists which do not appear to have taken this into consideration. In one year, for instance, *Dark of the Moon* was placed alongside *The Shoemaker's Holiday* and *The Beaux' Stratagem*. The discrepancy between these plays, on linguistic grounds alone, is surely too great for such a choice to be a fair one.

Unlike those following a literature syllabus drama candidates are not precluded from studying plays in translation. As an alternative to choosing plays from all periods of western European drama, it would be interesting to restrict the selection of texts to the advent of so-called 'modern' drama, that is from Ibsen onwards, and to insist that every candidate studied one play written in English and one in translation. The twentieth century has been one of the richest periods of drama in our history and the variety of experimentation ranges from sylized verse plays to a realistic exploration of social problems. It is vital to remember that theatre is a living force and some pupils will be better prepared for a study of texts written long ago if they have already encountered contemporary explorations of the same moral problems.

The O/A-level syllabus requires two plays to be studied from the same period which appears a sounder basis for study until one discovers that classical Greek and Roman Theatre is considered to belong to one period and that plays as disparate in background as *The Persians* by Aeschylus, and *The Pot of Gold* by Plautus, are grouped together. This is hardly a comparable alternative to *A Taste of Honey* and *The National Health*. As an alternative to the present system perhaps pairing could be made of plays from different traditions which are analogous in one important respect, such as theme, style or method of presentation. This would eliminate the inequalities of the present system and would be particularly valuable in demonstrating the influence of such seminal figures as Ibsen and Brecht.

At O- and O/A-level the knowledge of the set texts is examined by written paper. Besides this and the practical test each examination carries a third part. At O-level this is a selection of course-work, of which three pieces demonstrate the candidate's reactions to and reflections upon the work, and four of which are evaluations of productions the candidate has attended. The third part of the O/A-level is a project. In both exams the work differs only in quality from their CSE counterpart and is the clearest way in which work at one stage is encouraged to develop at another.

The written part of the A-level exam comprises an individual study researched in the candidate's own time and two very demanding written papers which test a knowledge of two set texts and the history of one substantial period in the development of European theatre, as well as a knowledge of at least one figure who influenced the theatrical traditions of his day. There is also a question designed to test the candidate's appreciation of dramatic techniques. This consists of a passage from an unseen play on which three questions must be answered on such aspects as mood, characterization, humour, language and the approach of actor and director. All these sections are admirable in themselves but it is tempting to wonder if the exam is not trying to cover too much and that it would be better if one or two of the parts were cut out or made alternatives to one another.

One thing is certain and that is that the time has already arrived when the whole structure of school examinations in drama should be the subject of a thorough and considered study by a national body. The piecemeal way in which it has developed has not led to coherence throughout the course. It is particularly regrettable that candidates following the present CSE drama courses have little chance to develop any of the decision-making skills which it fosters while they are still at school, though similar activities will be presented to them if they follow a course containing drama in a college of higher education. It is also to be hoped that a drama or theatre arts course will be available to all when the new 16-plus examinations are inaugurated. Perhaps by this time the unique methods of assessment established by the subject will have won wide enough recognition for them to be used in the examination of other areas of the curriculum. It would be especially appropriate to use an unrehearsed improvisation as part of the assessment in an integrated studies or humanities course. Another hope is that the willingness of examination boards to permit totally untried methods of assessment to be introduced will continue.

Many of the very first drama syllabuses were very vague in their objectives and what was produced was a pale shadow of a course designed for drama students at 18-plus. As a result pupils followed a stultifying course of theatre history unrelated to their own problems and the world they saw around them. It is still vital that all dramatic activities are seen as part of a vigorous and constantly developing process. As Professor Moses Finley said on the stage of our National Theatre in the 1979 British Museum Lecture:

The Greek heritage is the idea of a theatre. Their theatre was one such idea, the first one. That is credit enough. Hopeless attempts to reproduce it, or imitate it, do no honour to either the Greeks or their invention. [Finley 1980]

Whenever and wherever our subject is taught the basic aim must be to demonstrate that drama is a living force which provides society with the opportunity to be both creative and critical of itself.

9 *Theatre-in-education as a resource for the teacher*

Pam Schweitzer

In this chapter I shall be considering the relevance of the devising and performing process of a theatre-in-education company to the class teacher in a school. This will incidentally involve appraising the usefulness of theatre companies to teachers as consumers, but on the whole I am going to take this for granted from the outset. Rather, it will involve looking at theatre-in-education as a teaching strategy which is available for teachers to use for themselves. The glaringly obvious differences between the working conditions of a professional theatre company devising its own material and taking it from school to school, and the isolated class teacher pursuing a set curriculum within a single establishment might make such a premise look extremely tenuous, but I shall attempt to demonstrate that there are useful connections to be made between the two situations.

Like teachers in schools, theatre-in-education (TIE) teams set out to impart ideas and information to children in an accessible way. They seek to convey their content, their syllabus, through carefully chosen examples. These examples must be sufficiently developed and particularized to be interesting in themselves to the children, but they must also symbolize or represent the key concepts of the chosen learning area. The team's task is to enable the children to experience the significance of these concepts for themselves at their own level.

Unlike most teachers in schools, TIE teams physically represent their chosen examples for the children in the rich context of an elaborate fictitious situation. Inside the fiction, they assume roles which demonstrate conflict. The personalizing of conflict in this way enables the children to enter into a dialectical relationship with the learning material, to retain it vividly and to draw conclusions about it at their own level.

I shall be arguing that the process of devising situations and taking roles to carry content has potential significance for class teachers whatever their subject. But I, too, should perhaps proceed by example.

The programme I should like to feature was devised in 1977 for upper-junior and lower-secondary pupils (10- to 13-year-olds) in South London. It was called *Empire Made*, and was created and performed by the Greenwich Young People's Theatre in their Stage Centre in Woolwich.

Empire Made begins gently with a benign British business man holding up a perfectly ordinary plastic doll of the kind you can pick up for £1 in Woolworths, and explaining that he runs a factory in Hong Kong where these dolls are made. He chats to the children about how reasonable these products are, and how happy he is to be able to make available to them good quality toys at prices they can afford. He goes on to talk about what it is like to run a factory a long way from home in such a busy, over-crowded city as Hong Kong, but how it has its compensations in that the workers are friendly and willing, and there are beautiful places to live a little way out of the city over-looking the bay.

He introduces us to two of his workers, who turn out to be girls of approximately the same age as the audience, and leaves them to get on with their work, talking to us as they like. We watch the girls painting the dolls' faces very fast and skilfully. They talk to us and to each other as they do so. Gradually their appalling work schedules are revealed to us in a calm uncomplaining way, and we learn something of the difficulties faced by their families. There is no tearing at our heart-strings, but a simple catalogue of 'how it is'; what it is like to be a child worker in Hong Kong in 1977 making dolls for London children. The girls do not question their situation, apart from a little moan here and there over some point of detail, but there is a certain discernible discomfort on the part of their young audience as they compare this way of life with their own.

The action then moves into the home of one of the girls as she introduces us to her family and explains how they live. Their living quarters are extremely cramped, their old granny, who is not too well, lives with them, the father has difficulty earning money at all, and the young brother, whose studies they must all save up to pay for, is extremely discontented. Food is very basic, medical care is often unobtainable or too expensive, schooling for most is brief, and work is hard to come by unless you can bribe your way into the street market stall-holders' group or some such precarious livelihood.

These characteristics of life in Hong Kong are demonstrated in stretches of simple dialogue between members of the family, linked by direct narration to the audience by the girl. Settings are minimal (a few wooden boxes for the home scenes), movement is linear and functional, the interchanges between the characters are almost dia-grammatic. The action is punctuated by songs, mostly unaccompanied and sung in a direct 'out front' style but with a touch of the oriental in the harmonic arrangements. These songs comment on the action, and there is a slight change in the lighting so that the singers appear in silhouette; a device which obliges us to listen to the words rather than watch the performers. Nobody shouts about how dreadful things are in Hong Kong; the whole of the action merely demonstrates 'how it is'.

The inspiration for all this was clearly Bertolt Brecht. We feel some empathy for the characters, but we are not allowed to identify with them in a way which implies self-forgetfulness. On the contrary, the demonstration they offer us of their life is designed to cause us to reflect upon how different it is from ours and, implicitly, to begin to wonder why this should be so. In an interview in 1926 Brecht commented:

The production has got to bring out the material incidents in a perfectly sober and matter-of-fact way. The play's meaning is usually blurred by the fact that the actor plays to the audience's hearts. Contrary to the present custom, the figures portrayed ought to be presented quite coldly, classically and objectively. They are there to be understood.   [Willett 1977]

Towards the end of *Empire Made*, the girl's brother espouses the cause of revolution. He has studied Chinese Communism and he believes that it would be a better system for them than living under the British Empire as he experiences it and as we have witnessed it. He reads forbidden literature and has links with underground organizations. His family are extremely worried about the boy's involvement as it could jeopardize his progress (which is their only insurance for the future) and endanger their livelihood. They do not share his enthusiasm for communism or his belief that it could ever be made to work for their benefit in Hong Kong. The audience understand that even to read communist literature or meet with other communists is dangerous, and that the police and a strong spy network operate to make sure things stay as they are. The programme in no way advocates communism, and there is even criticism by other characters of communist philosophy and what it would mean for them in terms of possible greater hardship in the short term. *Empire Made* merely outlines the sort of circumstances in which communism might seem to offer an alternative, a possibility of change; that is where people live in poverty and have little to lose.

The toy factory owner rounds off the play in a somewhat self-satisfied manner, outlining the ways in which Hong Kong has benefited by the presence of British investors like himself, all of which now has a somewhat ironic ring for the children. He indicates that he hopes the people of Hong Kong will have their way, and that a further lease of Hong Kong to the British government will be granted when the present one runs out in a few years. There is a short discussion after the programme with the actors, and then the children leave the centre for their schools (on the day I saw the show, amidst excited enthusiastic chatter about what they had seen, in which their teachers joined).

Empire Made was a success on several grounds; first aesthetically, in that the visual and musical elements were most effective and the dialogue very strong, though so simple; second, emotionally in the understatement of the girl and her family, the simple resignation with which they described and lived their lives, and in the rebellion of the brother which was exciting and invigorating to behold; and third, intellectually, in that the structure was effective in forcing us to tangle with political and social problems of another group to whom we are linked by trade and profit. Let us now consider how and what the children in the audience learn in the course of watching and reflecting upon *Empire Made*.

The children know that what they are being shown is in some sense illusion. They are not in Hong Kong and these people are not doll-sellers or makers at all, but actors who are performing for them. The illusion has its own momentum and its own truth which the children as audience are committed to following through to its end. Through narration, dialogue, action and song, a set of characters are presented who live very differently from the children, and one of them seeks to communicate to them a complete picture of this life. She makes it happen for them, offering a demonstration of how it is, not a list of

161

complaints or slogans or a plea for help. The children watch, listen, feel sympathy even when it is not asked for, and they reflect. They are connected with the demonstration, partly by the flow of empathy, partly by their awareness that the girl is roughly their age ('there but for fortune') but lives a much harder life than they do, and partly by the ever-present Western-faced dolls which act as a powerful reminder that they, the audience, are somehow implicated in the fate of the characters before them.

Perhaps their reflections might take the following form:

'These children have to work such long hours for so little money, so that I, who come from a much richer family in a much richer country, can have my toys (which I suppose I could really do without, anyway) for a lower price. The girl who makes these toys probably does not have any toys of her own.'

As the play develops and more is learned of how the family live in Hong Kong, the reflections might continue along these lines:

'My mum and dad would not work for so little and we would not put up with such awful housing. I suppose if British people make dolls they want to be paid more money so they can have good homes, and so the dolls they make are more expensive and I couldn't afford to buy them. So I suppose I am glad that we've got Hong Kong and that I can get cheap dolls from there. . . . But I don't think it is right for children of my age to live like that. Perhaps these dolls are rather expensive in a roundabout sort of way after all.'

Much of this stream of consciousness, if it took place at all, might never be more fully verbalized than as follows: 'It's awful, isn't it? I really think it's wrong them having to work like that. Not that there's much we can do about it, except perhaps not buy Hong Kong dolls, and that won't help them much. Whatever they do, they'll have to do it themselves if it's going to change.' However, this play is recallable and the children can reflect upon it after the event with their teachers. By using the powerful symbol of the doll (and let us be clear that the children will give it the significance of symbol* – rich Britain and poor Hong Kong – as the play unfolds) the worlds of London and Hong Kong become inextricably linked for the audience, and the children are in a position to understand some of the economic and political implications of this relationship which would previously have been inaccessible to them. They have been given a glimpse of a world community where some labour for little so that others can have more for less.

I imagine that it was the company's aim to render accessible through symbolic representation the complex relationship between empire and exploitation in the light of the debate about child labour in Hong Kong and about the future of that colony when Britain's lease runs out in a few years' time. Bringing the children up sharply against a very different style of life for someone of their own age, engaging them sufficiently in that life for them to experience it (albeit vicariously) causes them to reflect on their own way of life and revise their view of it in the light of new evidence. This was perhaps the TIE team's curriculum, and they used their own tools to handle it so that a change in understanding could take place. To recapitulate, their tools were (*a*) story and character to carry the facts and ideas, (*b*) movement, music and settings to create impact and increase concentration, (*c*) a powerful symbol to hold the frame,† (*d*) illusion by which the children could be transported into another situation which would interest them and shed light on their own, (*e*) empathy which the company could arouse by relating the content of the programme to universally understood concepts such as home, hunger, fear, family, and (*f*) reflection which the company could stimulate by their detached playing style (as suggested by Brecht) and by incorporating narration and comment into the show and by the post-performance discussion between the company and the audience.

This programme would then pass into a rather different curriculum: that defined by the particular school. Junior schools would have a lot more lee-way to pursue the programme than secondary schools for obvious time-tabling reasons, but let us briefly consider the cross-curricular potential of *Empire Made*.

Margaret Sandra, Senior Teacher and head of English at a South East London school, who took a group of first year pupils to *Empire Made*, commented:

'The programme offered a very good entry into looking at changing conditions of childhood. We looked at how the class would have been

---

*† See SCYPT Journal (1980) no. 5, for two articles by Geoff Gilham and Gavin Bolton on use of symbol in education. * Gilham analyses how an object becomes an image and a symbol. † Bolton itemizes criteria for testing the effectiveness of a symbol (p. 5). It must 'Combine three important functions: (1) it provides a focus in action that encapsulates the thematic meaning of the topic, (2) it features the context in some way and (3) it engages the feelings of the participants'. The doll seems to me to measure up to these criteria very satisfactorily.

treated at different times in society, and how in many ways they live a treasured existence in comparison with even fifty or sixty years ago, and that they are sheltered from the harsh realities of survival. That raised a lot of questions about *why*, about *who* they are and what has brought about these changes. So we were able to achieve some kind of historical perspective, as well as looking at the current exploitation and the way in which their own consumerism actually oppresses people of their own age in another country.'

There are so many ways an imaginative teacher could pursue this programme, depending on the particular interests of the class concerned. One could follow the programme's own idea and look at other imported products which are part of our everyday life, tracing them back to their country of origin and finding out as much as possible about how they are produced and manufactured, under what conditions, and what the human/social implications are of the facts which emerge. One could draw comparisons between child labour in Hong Kong today and in nineteenth-century London, and look at how conditions gradually improved in this country and what brought about those improvements. One could focus on Hong Kong itself, and find out why Britain held the lease of this land so far away, what historical events threw it into our grasp, and consider what might have happened to it if this had not been its fate (the company providing some very useful background information on this theme, as I remember). One might look at other bits of the world which are marked in pink, or which were when their parents were at school, and consider how we came by them and what has happened to them since. One could set up factories in the classroom, perhaps two on contrasting lines, and play out life in a Hong Kong factory and life in a British factory with trade union representation and specified minimum wages and maximum hours. One could write the story of the brother in the play up to, and perhaps beyond, his arrest, taking into consideration his family's reactions and his sister's efforts to release him. Perhaps at a more sophisticated level, one could look at which British industries (such as Sheffield steel, electronics, clock and watch-making and toy-making to name but a few) are losing out to Hong Kong competition backed by British investors who might otherwise invest in their own country's industrial development, creating more jobs back home, instead of destroying them.

All these avenues, which could be labelled geography, history, drama, English and social studies respectively, were opened up by the programme. The thinking behind it and its impact, like so many TIE programmes, cut across curricular divisions. Even if none of these avenues were pursued by the teachers, the children assimilated and accommodated a challenging new perspective on what they already knew: that Hong Kong goods are cheaper, which would enable them to answer the question *why?* A TIE programme cannot rely for its impact on how far it connects with, or will be pursued across the curriculum (although teams who suggest avenues for follow-up almost always extend the life-span of the related work in the school), but rather on how far it connects with the child. Its impact is determined at the moment of meeting with its audience, and by how far they grasp the significance of the chosen set of symbolic images.

Theatre-in-education teams make their own curriculum, in that they determine their own areas of study independently of any other syllabus and in the light of an independent system of priorities. They have the freedom of artists to select their own content. Teachers may read this and feel only envy for such freedom, bogged down as they often are by the requirements of external exams or internally ordained programmes of work emanating from senior teachers in their own departments with whom they may be totally out of sympathy. But again I wish to establish the connection between the work of the TIE teams and that of the class teacher. Artists they may be, but they are artists in education and their task is to impart their vision whole to their young audiences. This involves translating adult perception into child-accessible perception, so that the children have at the end of the programme the same sense of its importance and significance for them as the TIE team had at the point when they committed themselves to it. They must render the (often difficult) content of the programme available to the children in a strong immediate manner by connecting it with what they already know. They cannot take the children's interest in, or desire to learn about, the content for granted, but must find ways for them to engage with the material by showing that it is part of something bigger, more universal, something which matters and which could come to matter to them in quite a personal way. This is not quite the same as child-centred learning, for the TIE team (like the subject teacher) determines content, rather than the children choosing it for themselves, but it does involve the team in plumbing beneath the surface of the content for both wider themes and more personal significance which will help the child to learn.

It was with these thoughts in mind that I approached teachers in the secondary school where I was working, to see how the TIE approach could be applied on a practical level in the classroom. Could history, social science, chemistry or geography teachers devise fictions and create roles which would allow pupils to connect personally with the wider themes underlying their school subjects? Could subject teachers stand back from their syllabus and try approaching the work tangentially through symbolic representation? Could teachers who are not actors take on roles and maintain them sufficiently to uphold the fictitious situation for their pupils? I was willing to work for an hour a week with any subject teacher who was interested in exploring this avenue, and it is worth mentioning straight away that a surprising number of people from a whole range of departments took up the offer. I shall describe one of the resulting experiments so that readers can judge for themselves how far we were successful.

In discussion with a chemistry teacher about the possible application of TIE methods to her field of work, we tried to see how the content (the study of chemicals) could be shown to have important universal implications and a personal significance for the pupils. We decided that the way forward was to look at what happens when a mineral is located in an area. What are the implications for those who find it, in terms of its usefulness, its danger, its profitability, and what are the implications for those who live near to where it has been found? Could we represent the potential conflict between these two groups in a way which would involve the pupils, and could we use role-play to do this?

We devised a scenario which could be enacted in the pupils' regular chemistry lesson, and we invited the head of the local teachers' centre, who happens to be a scientist and a sociologist as well as being a brave man with a sense of humour, to come to our school for the lesson and help us play out the fictitious situation. This was not going to involve great dramatic skill; merely the willingness to assume an attitude to a dilemma and to maintain it as though he truly held it for the purposes of clarity and reflection. I would arrange to be present at the chemistry lab on some pretext and adopt a contrasting attitude, and the chemistry teacher herself would adopt a third. She would begin a perfectly ordinary chemistry lesson which would then be interrupted by the visitor from the teachers' centre, and the pupils would be party to an apparently spontaneous discussion between us, in which they would speedily become involved. It was necessary to prepare certain props such as a suitable rock sample, a chart and some supplementary evidence in the form of a diary written by a local professor to give credibility to the fictitious situation we were setting out to create. The following is an account of what happened.

The visitor arrives in the classroom bearing a lump of rock which he explains he has unearthed near the school grounds where he has initiated a 'dig'. The teacher sets the pupils some work to do so that she can discuss this matter, though she expresses some reluctance at having her lesson interrupted. She introduces the visitor as the head of the teachers' centre and asks the girls to excuse her for a few minutes. They carry on with their work, but several listen in to the conversation between their teacher and the visitor. It emerges that he has unearthed something which looks to him significant, and he wants to use the laboratory and the services of the teacher whom he knows, to test it. He is following a hunch that it might connect with an important reference in a local diary from 1903 which he has recently stumbled upon which mentions the possibility of 'seizblend' (an element we invented for the purpose of the exercise) lying under this stretch of South-East London. He shows on a map where he thinks it runs, this important seam, taking in several of the streets around the school where the girls live. (We made sure this was the case by sending a copy of the class register with addresses to the person creating the map.)

The visiting enthusiast is in a state of high excitement because of his find and talks of getting the bulldozers into the area as soon as possible if the chemical tests confirm his suspicions. The chemistry teacher asks him to slow down a bit and consider the implications of his find. She does this at my behest, as I pick up what is happening and fear the consequences for people who actually live in the area. The girls are very gradually alerted to the fact that some disagreement is going on in the classroom and that it might concern them. They start listening hard. They want to know what this substance is and how it could be mined. The visitor explains that it could be the answer to neutralizing of some radioactive waste, but it is notoriously hard to mine, so all the houses and gardens near to the seam, and possibly the whole area, would have to be bulldozed before proper excavation could take place. It would be worth a fortune though, so there could of course be reasonable compensation.

At this stage the chemistry teacher divides the pupils (third years, aged 14- to 15-years-old) into groups to study the diary which the visitor has brought with him, the chart showing the estimated course of the seam under the area and showing their home streets crossing it,

167

and the sample itself. They are asked to consider how the sample might be tested in ways related to their own recent chemical experiments, and to consider the implications of this find. The three 'players' demonstrate different responses to the find. I argue that the discovery is bad news for everyone and is best forgotten and not referred to again, drawing their attention to its environmental and social implications. The chemistry teacher expresses great interest and feels that the subject should be fully explored for the furtherance of scientific knowledge, its social implications being more or less irrelevant for the moment. The visitor feels that it would obviously make his personal reputation and his fortune, would really put the area on the map, and might be a significant factor in our nuclear strategy.

The discussion gradually becomes general and more broad-ranging, with the girls playing an ever fuller part in it as they realize what is going on and how it might affect them. Some draw attention to the fact that the diarist of 1903 appeared to become ill shortly after coming into contact with this substance, and they fear that it might be dangerous to expose others to it. One or two are alarmed and refuse to touch the sample. There is much talk of moving out of the area, having to find new homes and whether one would be likely to receive adequate compensation. Discussion grows very lively with lots of hard questioning from the girls of their impulsive visitor.

In this manner, the pupils became involved with some of the universal issues and the personal implications which lie beneath the discovery of an important substance. We felt that we had been able to ask the questions which matter, such as: (*a*) Does science have social responsibilities? (*b*) Is there such a thing as pure science or does scientific study always have social implications which require public consultation and a measure of accountability? (*c*) Who should decide what is in the public good? And (*d*) is it better not to know about certain things? And we felt that we had been able to raise these questions by exploring the personal implications which go with them, such as: (1) How do we feel when the safety of our own home is under threat? (2) What recourse have we when our own area is going to be changed in ways beyond our control and against our wishes? (3) How can we argue on equal terms with experts who talk a scientific language, and are proposing things which we do not fully understand, but whose plans concern us and could harm us? (4) When these experts tell us things will work out well for us, should we trust them, and what can we do if we do not trust them to safeguard our own interests? And (5) do I really want to move away from my area now for the sake of some experiments, and will I be safe if I stay?

And so, in the most unlikely area of the curriculum, we found ways of using TIE methods for the greater involvement of the class in learning, by connecting the wider issues, whose significance they might not previously have grasped, with what was already understood by them and already felt to be important. We devised a fictitious situation, we used plot and evidence to create credibility, and we took roles to clarify conflicting attitudes and heighten the temperature of the discussion. The pupils were not aware that this was a 'set-up' event. It was 'Invisible theatre', to use the words of Augusto Boal in his fascinating study of the uses of theatre (Boal 1969, pp. 143–7), *Theatre of the Oppressed*, designed to promote full and free discussion of an important question in an artificially heightened atmosphere. I must say that the enjoyment this chemistry teacher, our teachers'-centre volunteer and I, derived from planning and executing this small programme was considerable and has certainly affected the ways in which we view each other's subjects.

I think it was important to the success of this experiment (and others like it undertaken in the school) that the enactive learning took place before the material was approached through more conventional methods, such as 'talk and chalk' sessions or 'reading around'. This meant that when other related work was approached it elicited a more positive response than might otherwise have been the case. The experiment served to connect TIE methods and the teaching of chemistry, but more importantly it served to connect pupils with content.

Margaret Sandra, the Senior Teacher to whom I referred earlier, is convinced of the value of this strategy. She comments:

'I think it would be ideal if teachers could adopt a TIE team approach to kick-off a theme or an idea. It would aid identification on the children's part, and generate greater effort into the rest of the work which would then come in from all directions, uniting history, social science, English, and so on. It would open up the curriculum and expose the inter-relationships of the teaching disciplines in a way which would be of benefit to all concerned, children and teachers alike. Children who participate in a TIE programme do not feel that they have to work very hard. At the same time, they learn a great deal more than perhaps eight disparate lessons could give them simply because they enjoy themselves, they are involved, they are able to identify, and they take away with them some very important notions.'

The chemistry experiment described above, and others of a similar nature conducted with teachers from different departments throughout the school, were put together in a tremendous hurry and really only happened at all because the school was enlightened enough to allow one hour's planning time for one member of the drama department to work with any subject teacher who happend to be free and who was feeling adventurous. We skated on surfaces and cut corners, but I think the children still benefited and took a fresh look at some of their school work as a result. All the events devised under this programme were repeatable, and several have been built into the teaching schedule for the coming year. This is a potential growth area for curriculum development, especially as experiments of this kind tend to develop their own momentum. They are stimulating in themselves and give teachers confidence in their own creativity and in the importance of the work they are doing in schools. All that is required of subject teachers who wish to take on the idea of devising their own 'programmes' is the willingness to think up relevant exemplary situations and assume roles inside them. Any teacher, just like any pupil, can soon find the confidence to try this, given a little support from people within the school, and it might pay dividends in terms of the increased interest and involvement of the pupils in the content of their lessons, especially as it requires the teachers to consider what really are the important issues underlying the syllabus content. The TIE perspective is one which is beneficial to the subject teacher and pupils and can fruitfully be borrowed to aid learning in schools.

10 Getting the best out of your drama adviser

Ken Byron

It is easy to scoff at drama advisers. Rather like college of education lecturers, they do not spend *all* their time in classrooms and are, therefore, liable to attack as being remote or as 'having no idea what it is all about'. Those who can't teach, teach teachers or go into advisory work?

A classic attack on drama advisers occurred not very long ago in *Outlook 10*. An anonymous contributor offered the following typology of drama advisers:

1 The Scorched Earth Adviser, or exponent of 'the dog in the manger' attitude. If teachers try anything that he or she hasn't initiated or isn't personally involved in (for example, starting a Saturday morning drama club for children in a particular area), then it is officially killed-off. Perhaps the subconscious feeling behind this is the insecurity that a teacher may create something better than the adviser could have done.

2 The Frustrated Actor Adviser, who is still on a kind of audience/actor ego trip. He or she has perhaps an adverse effect on schools and staffs. Rather than encouraging drama, the feeling that can be left is a hostile one, the teachers not wishing to touch drama if it means they have to adopt what for them is a very phoney lifestyle. They associate drama with superficiality and 'darlings'.

3 The Great Idea Adviser, who rushes about enthusing madly over a fantastic idea, moves heaven and earth in the initial inspiration, sets it up, gets people interested, and then enthusiasm and/or idea collapses, so nothing more happens. This is not encouraging or advising – it's more like a confidence trick.

4 The Office Boy Adviser, who rarely leaves his or her office, but is very hot on theoretical words, letters, articles. In short – a rubber stamp.

5   The Last Minute Adviser, who manages to administrate, arrange, organ-
ise or even arrive just in time to make the diplomatic face-showing, and
thereby preserves some shred of credibility to himself, if not to others.

6   The Play's-the-Thing Adviser. Instead of fostering and encouraging
drama for its own sake and seeing its value in terms of child development,
the building of relationships and everything else that drama can achieve, he
or she is ONLY interested in the amateur dramatics side of it, hoping it will
all produce some wonderful local amateurs. Happily this breed is dying
out.

7   The Real Drama Adviser. He or she is an open-minded adviser, who is
there giving encouragement; is available with assistance, money, resources
and information to schools and other concerned bodies; is leading, inspir-
ing and fostering; and is more often than not doing a magnificent job in the
face of a great deal of difficulty and criticism like this article!   [*Outlook*
1978]

I cannot deny having met some of the first six types on this list, but I
have met more who try earnestly to do the job to the best of their
abilities. The truth is that advisers (like teachers) vary widely in their
characters and abilities. Moreover their remit, their influence, their
freedom of manoeuvre, and the amount of time they are allowed to
spend on drama matters all vary tremendously from authority to
authority. I think, however, that there can be no doubt that drama is
more likely to thrive in an authority which has expressed its commitment to the subject by appointing an adviser to be responsible for it.

My aim here is twofold:

First, to present a brief *factual* outline of what drama advisers do, so
that teachers may have a better idea of what kind of creature it is they
are dealing with.

Second, to look in some detail at relations and contacts between
teachers and drama advisers *mainly from the teacher's point of view*,
asking the question: 'How can the teacher make the best use of his
drama adviser?' Throughout, the assumption will be that drama
advisers ought to assist not just drama specialists, but all teachers who
have an interest in drama, whether they teach in the primary, secondary, special, FE or HE sectors. There has been increasing awareness
over recent years of the wide applicability of drama methods across
the curriculum and I would see drama advisers as the main agents for
encouraging the use of such methods. Because I am not addressing
myself solely or even mainly to drama specialists, some of the things I

say may seem exceedingly obvious to some readers. My excuse is that what is obvious to them may never have occurred to others.

What drama advisers do

There is no one type of drama adviser but rather many kinds of advisers who have a responsibility for drama:

a Some authorities have no adviser responsible for drama.

b In some authorities drama is the responsibility of an adviser whose main concern is another curriculum subject, most commonly English.

c Other authorities have general advisers or inspectors, who combine a general brief (for example, for a geographical block of schools within the authority) with a specific responsibility for drama across the whole authority.

d Some have a specialist drama adviser, whose sole responsibility is for his subject.

e Others again have not only a specialist drama adviser, but also, under his direction, a team of advisory drama teachers (or perhaps a single advisory teacher).

f In a few cases (for example, where a drama adviser has left and not been replaced) there may be an advisory teacher or a team of advisory teachers who work, not to a specialist adviser, but to a general adviser or to another subject adviser.

It is obvious that teachers interested in drama are more likely to get direct help (such as teaching or advisory visits to their schools) from a specialist adviser and even more likely if that adviser has a team of advisory teachers at his disposal. But even if there is a specialist adviser in your authority, his work does not consist solely of working with teachers. An adviser's job is also to *advise the authority*. In other words some of his time is inevitably taken up with committee meetings, reports, budgeting etc. The specialist drama adviser is concerned with the FE, youth and community and adult education sectors, perhaps also with amateur theatre or with polytechnics and colleges of higher education, as well as with schools. He will also be responsible for the local education authority's links with local theatres and perhaps with developing, funding and supporting TIE work in local schools. Even in the school sector, as well as in-service and advisory visits, he has to deal with budgeting, with buildings and equipment. Drama studios get built because drama advisers fight for them in committees.

The job is an enormous one and inevitably advisers will specialize to some extent within the whole range of activities they are responsible for – either as a result of their own particular talents or inclinations, or of pressure from the director of education or chief education officer. In my view, a good adviser (of any subject) will do all he can to maximize the time he can spend on in-service work and advisory work in schools and colleges.

Using your drama adviser

So much for the drama adviser's job description! I shall turn now to the question of how teachers can use him. (When I use the term drama adviser I refer not simply to a specialist adviser but to anyone in an advisory position with a responsibility for drama, including advisory teachers. Obviously, many of the services teachers might expect, or hope for, are more easily provided by specialist advisers). I think the ways drama advisers can be of use to teachers fall broadly under 3 headings:

1 They can act as an information channel for teachers.
2 They can 'protect' teachers or be useful 'allies'.
3 They can be agents of in-service/personal and professional development for teachers/curricular developments within schools.

The adviser as information channel

Teachers should be able to look to drama advisers for advice and information on a whole range of topics. These include (in no particular order):

1 National curriculum developments relating to the teaching of drama.
2 Books to read to gain new ideas, material and ways of working.
3 Ideas for plays for the school production.
4 Appropriateness and quality of touring theatre groups offering schools performances.
5 Guidance for pupils who wish to pursue drama as a career, and

174

guidance for themselves in terms of career, professional development, secondment to appropriate full-time courses etc.

6   Where to see interesting drama work in other schools or colleges in the authority.

7   Expert guidance or help on technical aspects of drama/theatre – if not from the adviser himself, from someone else he recommends.

8   What kind of equipment to purchase (for example, lighting, sound equipment, staging etc.).

9   Where to buy or borrow equipment.

(Some drama advisers do much more than offer information on where to borrow equipment. They run costume wardrobes and keep a stock technical equipment which schools can hire from, usually at very low prices.)

No drama adviser will be able to answer immediately all the questions teachers ask him. But he is even less likely to be able to answer if they don't ask at all. Given the wider sphere in which he operates he should have a wide range of information available on many drama topics and if he doesn't have the answer to their question, he will probably be able to point them towards someone else who has.

The adviser as protector or ally

There may be occasions when a teacher feels himself or his work to be under threat: for example, developments in his school may occur which seem likely to affect the time, the space or the budget allocated to drama. Or there may be adverse reactions within the school to his teaching of drama in general, or to a particular production. In these kind of circumstances the drama adviser is his natural ally and the teacher would probably be wise to call upon his support. The adviser has two main advantages in such situations. The first is his status as adviser, i.e. as the representative of the director or CEO. The second is experience: he may well have dealt with similar situations in other schools before. For these reasons he may be able to negotiate or intervene upon the teacher's behalf, to some purpose, or at least offer sound advice on how to proceed. The same is true in more positive circumstances too: for example, where a teacher wants to press for new developments or expansion of drama within the school, the drama adviser can be a useful co-negotiator or behind-the-scenes-adviser. More generally any drama adviser worth his salt would respond readily if invited by a teacher to visit and discuss ways drama might develop in his school and how to get those developments implemented.

The adviser as agent of in-service work and curriculum and professional development

A few years ago, I posed the question in an article, 'What's wrong with drama training?' (Byron 1977) And I quoted an unpublished report by the National Association of Drama Advisers which gave the results of a survey of training institutions offering drama main courses. Among its conclusions were:

iv   The main body of work for B.Ed. was either theatre-based or literature-based.

v   Many colleges indicated that practical educational considerations were the concern of main courses (which B.Ed. students had been involved in) and not B.Ed. courses.

    BUT –

vi   85 per cent of main courses were also either theatre-based or literature-based.

vii   Many colleges, including some who had answered as indicated in (*v*), indicated that practical educational considerations were the concern of curriculum courses.

viii   All colleges who ran B.Ed. or main drama courses, also ran curriculum courses, but students on B.Ed. or main did not always take the curriculum course.

ix   Of the colleges not offering B.Ed. or main drama from whom replies were received, 65 per cent did not offer curriculum courses either.

x   I only discovered *one* college where *all* students did curriculum drama.

xiii   Most teachers of drama from colleges of education, therefore, have learnt about acting techniques, production techniques, stage management techniques, the history of the drama and theatrical representation, and – a few lucky ones – about children's theatre and/or history of drama and poetry, play analysis, dramatic criticism and appreciation, but have not had enough time to do any of these in much depth – and perhaps a consideration of child play, drama as a teaching aid.

xiv   It is very clear that few students experience at their own level what one would expect them to be helping children to experience in schools. They will have paid little consideration to the nature of drama as a means of learning and developing, rather than as something to be learned and developed. Nothing much will have been done to develop their own resources, their sensitivity, imagination, and perception. If their work in 'theatrical acting' was done in reasonable depth, the one saving grace might be that acting requires the same human qualities and sensitivities as teaching – but it would help if, through drama, drama specialists were helped more readily to relate these qualities to children.

xv . . . Colleges do not yet, on the whole, acknowledge that drama in education can be a main course as well as theatre or dramatic literature.

Since the NADA report considerable institutional change has gone on in teacher training: notably the shift from monotechnic to polytechnic institutions and from college certificates to degrees. The report is then very much out of date. But I think many teachers and advisers would agree with me that its main conclusions (that drama courses in teacher training are generally academic or performance-based, rather than classroom-oriented) are *even more true now* than when the survey was carried out. The polytechnic/degree shift has tended to decrease still further the time given to preparing student teachers directly to use drama with children.

This general lack of adequate preparation for the classroom means that most teachers are going to be in need of help, new ideas and a boost to their teaching confidence quite early in their career. The need for in-service work is intensified by the poverty of pre-service preparation.

The drama teacher's need for support is further intensified by his characteristic isolation. Often in secondary schools there will only be one drama specialist. In most primary and special schools and many secondary schools there is no drama specialist as such, but a teacher or two with a strong interest in developing drama. Specialist and non-specialist drama teacher alike will tend to lack anything more than very general support from within the school. So they will need to look outside the school for the opportunity to discuss their problems and successes with someone of similar interests, and the drama adviser has an important role to play simply as someone who 'understands'. During the years I taught in secondary schools, I valued greatly the occasion when my drama adviser came, because there was the opportunity to do some 'shared thinking' and to let a sympathetic colleague see some of my work and offer constructive comments.

Adviser–teacher contacts

The drama adviser's contact with teachers will tend to be through:

1 In-service courses
2 Teachers' groups or joint projects
3 Advisory/teaching visits to schools

Before looking at each of these in turn I want to offer what I believe are some important general observations about adviser–teacher contacts.

Drama advisers should be responders as well as initiators. In my view, drama in an authority will be the poorer where the adviser is the sole initiator. From the adviser's point of view it is very wearing and discouraging to have to provide all the new ideas. From the teacher's point of view it is inefficient: all the advisory initiatives in the world (new courses etc.) may be of no use at all if they do not relate to his interests and needs. Drama advisers have a responsibility to ask teachers what their needs and interests are. But teachers also have a responsibility to make them known to their adviser. One drama adviser said to me, 'I work best when demands are made on me'. A felt and expressed need is a very positive stimulus to action. So my advice to teachers is: Pester if you want to get the best out of your drama adviser.

I have said already that teachers need support from their drama adviser. I also think that they need him to challenge them and that they should expect this of him. By way of example, let me return to my own adviser's visits to the schools I taught in. What was valuable was not just the sympathetic ear but his constructive criticisms of the lessons or production he had seen and his suggestions for development. Of course such criticisms and suggestions were offered in the context of a relationship of mutual friendship, trust and respect. Indeed they *can* only be offered in such a context. If a drama adviser is to be of much use to a teacher, they must get to know each other.

There are a number of factors which can impede the growth of a relationship between adviser and teacher. A simple personality clash is one. Another is the adviser's 'Janus-like' role: he advises teachers, but he also advises the authority. He visits schools to offer professional support, but on other occasions he visits schools to inspect or evaluate. The extent to which advisers have 'inspecting' powers or functions varies between authorities, but all advisers have a substantial administrative role and can in some sense be seen by teachers as 'alien', 'powerful' or 'evaluating'. Advisers are often involved to some extent in appointments and promotions in schools. They also usually have a role in deciding whether or not novice teachers succeed in their probationary period – so if an adviser comes to see a probationary teacher work, there is bound to be some element of tension in the visit. The advisory drama teacher is less of a Janus-figure than the adviser proper. His work tends to be concentrated at the in-service/support end of the spectrum of advisory activities and so he is a less complicated figure to relate to.

Strange though it may seem, the drama adviser sometimes relates less successfully to drama specialists (particularly experienced ones) than to non-specialist teachers. The latter will tend to value his experience and expertise. The drama specialist on the other hand, may have as much experience and expertise as the adviser (or more), so he may ask 'What does this adviser have to offer that I don't already know?'. Or the adviser can feel inhibited from offering help or advice by the knowledge that a specialist is just as experienced as himself. Both are mistaken, I think, in believing that the adviser may have little or nothing to offer. Surely two experienced drama specialists always have something to learn *from each other* (even if one is teacher and the other his adviser)? Here I think it is the adviser's responsibility to find ways of relating to his experienced specialists on a basis of co-operation and equality rather than 'adviser' and 'advisee' – of which more later. And I would hope the drama teacher could respond to such overtures as an opportunity rather than as a threat to his status as an experienced specialist.

1 *In-service courses*

These are of many different kinds and a sensible drama adviser will put together as full and varied an in-service programme as possible, recognizing that different kinds of courses meet different kinds of need. Experienced teachers of drama will have different requirements of a course than a drama novice. One frequent complaint I have heard from experienced teachers is that, 'All drama courses concentrate on how to *begin* teaching drama'. Courses will be needed on the broad central area of classroom drama work (in itself multi-faceted) but also on production and technical matters, on links with other subjects and so on. As well as courses which develop their skills and knowledge as teachers, there is a need for some courses which allow teachers to work at their own level in drama and refresh themselves in that way. The one-day course is often a 'taster' – an introduction to drama for the interested but inexperienced – or to a new aspect of drama work for the rather more experienced. Or it may be an opportunity to bring in an outside tutor who can demonstrate new ways of working or bring an alternative perspective to that of the adviser himself.

Courses lasting 2 or 3 days or more, particularly residential courses, offer the chance for deeper penetration of the subject matter of the course, for the development of group identity and cohesion and consequently for a considerable increase in the energy levels of the participants. I think that advisers should offer as many residential courses as circumstances in their authority will permit, because the residential course permits a concentration of effort and sharing of experiences and viewpoints not otherwise easily achieved.

Short courses (say 1 to 5 days) offer teachers an opportunity to take a plunge: to get to know their adviser and introduce themselves; to familarize themselves sufficiently with an approach, technique or way of working to get themselves started or to develop their teaching a little further. Their problem is that they are short and that they end abruptly. It is best if teachers can have some form of follow-up support after short courses. Ideally advisory/teaching visits to their schools. Another solution to the 'cut-off' problem of the short course I have found to be useful, where numerous advisory school visits are not a viable follow-up, is to break short courses into two parts, some weeks apart. Part one prepares teachers to try things out in their schools; part two gives them the opportunity to report back, to reflect together on problems and successes, and to work out on the basis of these initial experiences what for them will be the soundest way of proceeding in the future.

Longer courses meeting, say, weekly over a term or a year, mean that the process of preparation, trying out, reporting back, re-evaluating and reshaping one's teaching can be carried out repeatedly over a substantial period of time. The long course gives the opportunity to pursue things in greater depth, and/or to pursue more aspects of drama teaching.

The in-service course is an essential aspect of curriculum and professional development. It is a period of withdrawal, however brief, from the pressure of daily teaching, which gives the opportunity to consider new approaches or how to deepen existing approaches. But I do not think it can be seen as anything like a complete programme for professional and curriculum development. For one thing, the very structure of a course tends to place the adviser in the role of 'expert' and teachers in the role of the 'ignorant to be instructed'. Teachers' groups or joint projects of one kind or another offer the chance for adviser and teachers to work together in less hierarchical and more informal, but equally fruitful ways. As suggested earlier these might be of particular relevance to experienced drama teachers.

2 *Teachers' groups and joint projects*

One drama adviser I know recently invited teachers in his authority to form working parties on 'infant drama', 'junior drama' and 'secondary drama'. The task of each of these working parties was to draw up a booklet offering guidelines for drama teaching in its own specific age-group. This project meant that teachers had the opportunity not merely to learn from the adviser but from each other and to contribute their own experience, skills and understanding to a tangible and worthwhile end-product. In making this offer the adviser was explicitly affirming his respect for his teachers' work and views – something that perhaps not all advisers do.

Joint drama festivals or productions in which several or many schools participate can be another way in which, in a different area, similar mutual learning and support between teachers can occur.

In many education authorities there is a local drama teacher's association, often affiliated to a national drama association. In my view, drama advisers ought to welcome these, make use of and work with them. I have heard a drama adviser complain that, 'These associations are trying to do the adviser's job for him.' My reply would be to suggest that the job is a big enough one for the adviser to welcome some help with it. In a number of authorities I am familiar with, the drama adviser has responded very positively to the existence of a local association and has, for example, been very ready to mount courses which his association has requested. Such an association provides a natural, ready-made framework within which teachers can meet and learn from each other. It also provides an easy mechanism for articulating the in-service needs of local teachers, as seen by the teachers themselves. A local drama teacher's association can, I think, considerably help non-specialist advisers, category (*b*), who will not usually have any particular personal expertise in drama to fulfil his in-service role towards teachers of drama.

3 *Advisory/teaching visits to schools*

These constitute the third essential strand in a really adequate overall in-service programme. Courses allow teachers a period of withdrawal to reflect on their practice; teachers' groups offer the opportunity to learn from other teachers; but it is in the school itself that the results of in-service work must show themselves. I think teachers have a right to expect their drama advisers to come into schools and teach, either solo or in collaboration with the teacher, and also to watch the teacher at work and to offer advice and constructive comments. An adviser who will not teach in schools, or who does so very rarely, cannot expect to retain his credibility with his teacher-colleagues. Of course, these remarks apply only to adviser categories (*c*) to (*f*). It would be unrealistic to expect someone in category (*b*), who is only concerned with drama as a very minor part of his responsibilities and who probably has little or no drama expertise, to fulfil this function.

Unlike courses and teachers' groups, advisory/teaching visits to schools can be tailored specifically to the particular teacher's need and to the context within which he works. Here I think lies their real value.

If there is to be actual value in such visits, both adviser and teacher need to be open-minded and willing to learn. If the teacher watches the adviser teach (or *vice-versa*) with the attitude: 'Now we'll see how inept/wrongheaded he is', few positive results are likely to emerge. The adviser must be responsive to the needs (spoken and unspoken) of the teacher. He must be willing to learn himself – even from watching/working with the most inexperienced teacher. The teacher, as I have already said, must look for challenge, as well as support, from the adviser. If an adviser's comments on a lesson amount to no more than 'Yes, that was very nice', it can hardly be said that the teacher has benefited very much.

I want now to look briefly at some of the different forms that an adviser's visits to work with a teacher can take, looking at the opportunities in each.

a *The adviser watches the teacher teach* This accompanied by discussion, gives the adviser a clear picture of the teacher's thinking and practice and of how he can best help that teacher. Of course, some teachers will be reluctant to allow the adviser to watch their work (especially at first), because of lack of confidence, or because they do not yet know the adviser well enough. This is fair enough, but I think it is essential that, at some point, teachers become willing to expose their drama work to the observation of a sympathetic colleague. The feedback they will gain about their practice from an observer can be invaluable. When an adviser does observe a teacher at work, he needs to observe intently and precisely, not casually and generally. He should avoid jumping too quickly to too many value judgements about the work. Before he can come to a real assessment of the work, he will need to question the teacher about, for example, the intention behind certain teaching acts, and his perception, as a teacher, of some incidents in the lesson. The adviser will need to offer challenge in his comments but from a basis of support for the teacher's work. And he should offer some guidelines for (or better help the teacher to clarify his own thoughts about) future development of the teacher's skill, work with a particular class or whatever other issues are raised. Such guidelines need to be appropriate to the teacher's personality, confidence and stage of professional development, as well as to the school context in which he works.

Advisers need always to remember that they are *advisers* and that ultimately the teacher has the right and the freedom to reject their advice.

b *The teacher watches the adviser teach* This is obviously a less threatening situation for the teacher than having the adviser watch him teach. It has its dangers. A demonstration lesson by an 'expert' can be off-putting for an inexperienced teacher – 'I know I could never do that!' or it can be off-putting to any kind of teacher if the aims/teaching style/strategies etc. are not reasonably congruent with his own. These dangers are greatest if the adviser does not know his teacher.

The main advantages I can see in the adviser teaching, while the teacher watches, are:

1 It establishes the adviser in the teacher's eyes as a colleague, a fellow-teacher, someone who 'knows what it's all about'.

183

2 Doing drama is always clearer and better than talking about it, and by teaching a lesson the adviser is able to make concrete and comprehensible ways of working he wishes to introduce to the teacher.

3 One of the keys to teacher development is that the teacher should be able to analyse his own work as clearly and objectively as possible. I think an adviser, when teaching a lesson for the benefit of a teacher, should ask that teacher to observe precisely and not generally. He might, for example, ask the teacher to observe the variety of teaching registers he employs in the course of the lesson (and note down the transition points), or the patterns of interaction among the pupils, or one of many other possible things. The choice of what to observe needs to be closely related to the teacher's own professional preoccupations and needs. By asking the teacher to observe precisely, by discussing his observations with him, the adviser can use his demonstration lesson to help the teacher sharpen his powers of lesson observation and analysis, and encourage him to employ these powers on his *own* work.

c *Adviser and teacher team-teach* This has the substantial advantage that teacher and adviser are placed on an equal footing as colleagues in a shared enterprise. One of the best ways to learn from a colleague is to share with him the process of planning, teaching and subsequent analysis, leading into further planning. I know of no better way of exposing and developing one's thinking and practice.

The three kinds of teaching visit above are not listed in any order (either hierarchical or sequential). One of them will be more appropriate to a particular need and relationship and time than the others. Sometimes one will lead naturally to another.

d *Non-teaching visits* Sometimes the teacher may wish simply to spend time in conversation with his adviser, trying to clarify his own mind and seeking advice about recent problems and successes in his teaching and plans for the future.

I have tried to provide information about what a drama adviser is and does, advice about how teachers can best make use of their adviser, together with some consideration of the advisory process from the advisory point of view. Ultimately it is up to teachers and advisers to make the process work. Arrogant or complacent teachers or ones who are content to repeat endlessly tired routines learnt many years before at college, are unlikely to benefit from an adviser's efforts. Conversely, the adviser who is self-important or narrow in his prejudices or who has time only for ideas or projects *he* has initiated is unlikely to have much to offer his teachers. If the advisory process is to be effective, both parties need to maintain an attitude of mutual trust, respect and openness and above all to remember that what passes between them is for the purpose of enriching the experience of the young people they are both paid to educate.

Postscript: Curriculum change and professional development

Jon Nixon

One thing is clear from the foregoing debate: the problem of how drama should relate to the whole curriculum cannot be reduced to the simple expedient of applying a set of drama teaching techniques across subject boundaries. The approach advocated by the contributors to this symposium demands a more sensitive response. At the heart of the endeavour is a concern with curriculum change through the professional development of teachers. In this brief postscript I shall mention three aspects of extended professionalism which have been highlighted in previous chapters.

Collaboration

Almost all the contributors have stressed the importance of collaboration as a basis for developing drama across the curriculum. Various kinds of collaborative learning have been documented: between pupils and the teacher in the classroom, between colleagues working within different areas of the curriculum, and between the school and a number of external agencies. In each case it is the quality of the relationship between the different parties – its capacity for equal partnership and sensitivity to the other's needs – that really counts.

The work documented in the central section of the book, in Part Two, demonstrates the importance of the role of teacher as bridge-builder between the school and its pupils. The classroom only becomes a meeting ground for cultures through the careful negotiation by the teacher of a relationship which endows with significance

187

the ideas and language of the child. In this process of negotiation the materials that are used and the way in which they are introduced and explored through drama play a vital part. No text is a closed book in drama. Every sentence is life.

Relationships between colleagues are a no less important aspect of the collaborative venture reported in the previous pages. Clearly, the ethos of the school and, in particular, the style of leadership adopted by the head determine to a very large extent the degree and quality of interchange between the individuals in any one institution. Terry Jones's note of cautious realism is a timely reminder that drama teachers cannot afford to wait for an ideal plot in which to cultivate their more exotic blooms. They must work with the soil that is beneath their feet. Having said this, however, it is also important to impress upon heads, deputy heads and directors of study that teachers – regardless of how skilled and inspired they may be – cannot win against a rigid and inflexible timetable.

Nor can they win against outside agencies that refuse to enter into genuine dialogue with them. The final section of this book has shown how a number of these agencies – the examining boards, theatre-in-education companies and local education authority advisory services – can be used to support drama work across the curriculum. The effectiveness of this support depends upon the mutual awareness of the constraints under which each is operating. In the present economic climate the chance of bringing about any radical change in the curriculum – given even the most sympathetic support – may well be minimal. The fault, however, is neither that of the outside agencies nor of the teaching profession they seek to serve. All those who are in any way connected with schools are suffering the disastrous consequences of government policies on public spending.

The curriculum cannot be defined solely in terms of what is learned and how. It must also be defined in terms of the context in which that learning takes place. Relationships in the classroom, in the school and in the wider social setting not only frame, but inform, the act of learning. The teacher is the nexus. Changing the curriculum necessarily involves increasing teachers' awareness of themselves as agents of change within a system which, although imposing a steely mesh of constraints, is not entirely self-determining. The task for the teaching profession is to accommodate where possible and resist where necessary. The two faces of collaboration: complicity and solidarity. Both are necessary.

Evaluation

One way in which teachers are able to gain the kind of increased self-awareness to which I have just referred is through the evaluation of their own practice. By adopting a more critical approach to their work they are able to improve their own performance in the classroom, develop or modify their theory of teaching, and communicate problems and insights to colleagues. In my previous book *A Teacher's Guide to Action Research* (Nixon 1981) I explored this particular aspect of extended professionalism in some detail. It is worth mentioning again, however, since the records of work contained in the present book testify to the importance of teacher self-evaluation in any serious attempt at developing drama across the curruculum.

Teaching, it would appear, can be very like driving a car in heavy traffic. The teacher, like the motorist, is constantly faced with unforeseen situations which demand a response. Some sort of a decision has to be made, even if it is the decision to do nothing. Classroom evaluation helps the teacher negotiate the unexpected – the sharp bends and concealed entrances – by informing the decision-making process. It makes apparent the teaching acts, unearths them and calls them to question.

Self-evaluation may also bring about an elaboration or synthesis of one's theory of teaching and learning. The live tradition emerging in the work of, say, Peter Chilver or Elyse Dodgson is not grasped from the air. It is grounded in the reality of the classroom. Their insights are generated by careful analysis of specific cases. The problems that concern them are empirically observed, not imported into the classroom from some bookish excursion into the educational hinterland. Their pedagogy is derived from their practice.

Clearly, if teachers intend to take the initiative in curriculum development they must be able to interpret their work to others. Classroom enquiry can lend substance to these crucial attempts at communication. Pupils, employers and parents are but a few of the stakeholders in the educational process. Changing the curriculum necessarily involves changing people's perceptions of what constitutes relevant knowledge and how this knowledge might be transmitted. The teaching profession must repossess its Socratic heritage. It exists that the age might question its own assumptions.

By stressing the importance of self-evaluation I am not suggesting that the problems with which schools are faced can find their ultimate

189

solution in the classroom. Far from it. Teachers cannot reduce the lengthening dole queue or provide adequate social services. All they can do is create in the context of their own classrooms some of the conditions necessary for broad social change. If that is worth doing – and I believe it is – it is worth doing well. Insofar as classroom evaluation helps the teacher in this task it should be seen as a valuable means of professional self-development.

Innovation

One of the assumptions underlying all the contributions to this book is that pupil needs must be met, in part at least, by a willingness on behalf of teachers to adopt an experimental approach to their work. For innovation to be effective, however, it must involve changes in perception as well as in practice. The important thing in mounting any innovative programme of work is to grasp the dynamic relation between curriculum content, teaching methods and the organization of the school as a whole. What is needed is not only a synoptic view of the curriculum, but a view of the school as a complex social setting framed by curricular concerns.

Questions concerning curriculum content are particularly pressing for the drama specialist. In the absence of any clear consensus as to the purpose of drama in schools, the responsibility for deciding what should be taught lies with the individual teacher. If drama is not about producing plays, what is it about? Gavin Bolton's answer is unequivocal. Educational drama, he argues, is primarily concerned with dramatic form. In the work of Elyse Dodgson we see a clear working out in practice of this credo. Drama becomes a means of exploring social issues insofar as it is handled as an art form.

Teachers of, say, history who wish to make use of drama in their lessons are faced with a different question. Their concern is with teaching methods rather than curriculum content. The history teacher knows what it is she wants to teach. The question is how she should teach it. As John Fines has shown, the knack is in gradually easing oneself and one's pupils into the drama mode through one's feeling for, and knowledge of, one's own discipline. Within the context of the history lesson the drama is only important insofar as it allows the child to be more, not less, of an historian. The drama must never be allowed to swallow the history.

It is within the context of the pastoral curriculum that the need for innovation is felt most acutely. Since the pastoral oversight of pupils is the responsibility of every teacher, Leslie Button's chapter represents a major contribution to our thinking about drama and the whole curriculum. He rightly stresses the need to understand the influences which, although strictly speaking non-curricular, shape the attitudes of pupils and teachers in schools. Drama is one way in which these influences can be brought to the surface and made explicit. It enables teacher and pupils to study the subtext of their own social relations.

Innovation is not something that just happens. It must be made to happen. As we have seen, the willingness of teachers is a crucial factor in the development of innovative practice in schools. Teachers, however, cannot go it alone. Without provision for inservice education and training, improved conditions of service, and adequate space and resources, any attempt at curriculum change is bound to be minimal in its impact. There is growing evidence that the current vogue for local and school-based curriculum research and development is being viewed as a cheap option by a number of agencies. It is high time that policy-makers learned to put their money where their mouth is.

All the contributors to this volume are located at the intersection of the three lines of professional development which I have briefly sketched: *collaboration*, *evaluation* and *innovation*. The map upon which these lines are traced is no less than society itself. Schools do not exist in a political vacuum. The curriculum of tomorrow is framed by the yesterday of Brixton and Toxteth, of Hackney and Bristol. It is shaped by the expectations of those who stand in the lengthening dole queue. No school is an island. No teacher is autonomous.

Who, then, will benefit from the development of a whole-school approach to drama? First, *teachers* will benefit. The cross-fertilization of ideas between disciplines and the opening-up of new and exciting areas of expertise is an inevitable consequence of such an approach. Second, the *school* will benefit from a reappraisal of the principles and practices of its entire curriculum. Third, and most important of all, the *pupils* will benefit from livelier and more varied lessons and a collaborative and experimental approach to teaching. A cross-curricular policy towards drama in schools is no longer an optional extra. It is a professional duty.

191

Bibliography

Allen, J. (1979), *Drama in Schools: its Theory and Practice*, Heinemann

Arcana, J. (1979), *Our Mothers' Daughters*, Berkley, California: Shameless Hussy Press

Barnes, D. (ed.) (1968), *Drama in the English Classroom*, National Council of Teachers of English, papers relating to the Anglo-American Seminar of the Teaching of English at Dartmouth College, New Hampshire

Bernstein, H. (1978), *For their Triumphs and For their Tears: Women in Apartheid South Africa* (revised edition), International Defense and Aid Fund (104 Newgate St., London EC1)

Boal, A. (1969), *Theatre of the Oppressed*, Pluto Press

Bolton, G. (1977), 'Creative drama as an art form', *London Drama*, vol. 5 no. 6

(1978), 'The concept of "showing" in children's dramatic activity', *Young Drama*, vol. 6 no. 3

(1979), *Towards a Theory of Drama in Education*, Longman

Brownmiller, S. (1975), *Against Our Wills: Men, Women and Rape*, New York: Simon & Schuster

Bruner, J. (1966), *Towards a Theory of Instruction*, Harvard: Belknap Press

Button, L. (1974), *Development Group Work with Adolescents*, Hodder & Stoughton

(1981), *Group Tutoring for the Form Teacher*, Hodder & Stoughton

Byron, K. (1974), 'Drama – subject or method?', *London Drama*, vol. 2 no. 1

(1977), 'Fit to teach drama?', *Young Drama*, vol. 5 no. 7

Cantarow, E. (1980), *Moving the Mountain: Women Working for Social Change*, New York: The Feminist Press and McGraw Hill

Chilver, P. (1978), *Teaching Improvised Drama*, Batsford

Chilver, P., and Gould, G. (1982), *Learning and Language in the Classroom: Discursive Talking and Writing Across the Curriculum*, Pergamon

Clegg, D. (1973), 'The dilemma of drama in education', *Theatre Quarterly*, vol. 3 no. 9

Cook, H. C. (1917), *The Play Way*, Heinemann

Crompton, J. (1973), 'A syllabus for drama?', *Young Drama*, vol. 1 no. 3

Curtis, B., and May, W. (eds.) (1978), *Phenomenology and Education: Self-Consciousness and its Development*, Methuen

Davies, M. L. (ed.) (1978), *Maternity: Letters from Working Women*, Virago

Department of Education and Science (1967), *Drama*, Education Survey 2, Her Majesty's Stationery Office

(1975), *A Language for Life*, Report of the Committee of Inquiry under the chairmanship of Sir Alan Bullock, FBA, Her Majesty's Stationery Office

(1977), *Curriculum 11-16*, Working Papers by Her Majesty's Inspectorate: a Contribution to Current Debate, Her Majesty's Stationery Office

(1981), *The School Curriculum*, Her Majesty's Stationery Office

Deverall, J. (1975), 'Drama: subject and service', *Young Drama*, vol. 3 no. 1

(1979), 'Public medium, private process: drama, child-centred education and the growth model of human development', unpublished MA (Ed) dissertation, University of Durham

Ehrenreich, B., and English, D. (1976), *Witches, Midwives and Nurses*, Writers and Readers Publishing Co-operative

Esland, G. (1971), 'Teaching and learning as the organisation of knowledge', in M. F. D. Young, *Knowledge and Control*, Collier-Macmillan, 1971

Findlay-Johnson, H. (1911), *The Dramatic Method of Teaching*, Nisbet

Fines, J., and Verrier, R. (1974), *The Drama of History*, Clive Bingley

Finley, M. I. (1980), *The Idea of a Theatre: the Greek Experience*, British Museum Publications

Friday, N. (1979), *My Mother, Myself*, Fontana

Gillham, G. (1974), 'Condercum School Report', for Newcastle-upon-Tyne LEA (unpublished)
    (1977), 'Drama and the integrated curriculum', *Young Drama*, vol. 5 no. 3

Goffman, E. (1974), *Frame Analysis*, Penguin Books

Harris, K. (1979), *Education and Knowledge*, Routledge & Kegan Paul

Hirst, P. (1967), 'Logical and psychological aspects of teaching', in R. S. Peters, (ed.) *The Concept of Education*, Routledge & Kegan Paul (1976 edn)

Holmes, E. (1911), *What Is and What Might Be*, Constable

Huie, H. W. (1980), 'My mother's arms', quoted in C. N. Davidson and E. M. Broner, *The Lost Tradition: Mothers and Daughters in Literature*, New York: Frederick Ungar

Johnson, L., and O'Neill, C. (ed.) (1982), *Selected Writings of Dorothy Heathcote*, Hutchinson

Lloyd-Evans, G. (1974), 'Crossroads for drama', *Young Drama*, vol. 2 no. 2

Maslow, A. (1974), 'What is a taoistic teacher?', in L. J. Rubin (ed.), *Facts and Feelings in the Classroom*, Ward Lock Educational

McGregor, L., Tate, M., and Robinson, K. (1977), *Learning Through Drama*, Heinemann

Nixon, J. (ed.) (1981), *A Teacher's Guide to Action Research*, Grant McIntyre

Norman, J. (1981), 'Why does teacher always get the best parts?', *The Times Educational Supplement* (17 July)

National Association for the Teaching of Drama, (1979), *The Development of Drama Teaching*, recommendations arising from the NATD conference at York University, January 1979
    (1980), *Drama in Education: the 1980s*, report of the NATD conference at Queen's College, Oxford, March 1980

Oakley, A. (1979), *Becoming a Mother*, Martin Robertson

Oeser, O. A. *et al.* (1962), *Teacher, Pupil and Task*, Tavistock

Outlook 10 (1978), journal of the National Association for Drama in Education and Children's Theatre (spring)

Parker, R., and Mauger, S. (1976), 'Self starvation', *Spare Rib*, no. 28

Peters, R. S. (1967), 'What is an educational process?', in *The Concept of Education*, Routledge & Kegan Paul (1976 edn)

Pick, J. (1973), 'Five fallacies in drama', *Young Drama*, vol. 1 no. 1

Plath, S. (1975), 'Three women: a poem for three voices', in *Winter Trees*, Faber & Faber

Porter, D. (1977), Editorial in *Outlook*, vol. 9 no. 3

Postman, N., and Weingartner, C. (1971), *Teaching as a Subversive Activity*, Penguin Education Special

Pring, R. (1976), *Knowledge and Schooling*, Open Books

Reeves, M. P. (1979), *Round About a Pound a Week*, Virago

Reid, L. A. (1980), 'Art: knowledge-that and knowing this', *British Journal of Aesthetics*, vol. 20 no. 4 (autumn), pp. 329–39

Richardson, E. (1966), *The Environment of Learning*, Routledge & Kegan Paul

Robinson, K. (1975), 'Find a space', (unpublished), University of London Examination Department

(ed.) (1980), *Exploring Theatre and Education*, Heinemann

Rogers, C. (1961), *On Becoming a Person*, Constable

Ross, M. (1975), *Arts and the Adolescent*, Schools Council Working Paper 54, Evans/Methuen Educational

(1978), *The Creative Arts*, Heinemann

Schools Council (1972), *Drama in Schools*, report of conference of the Schools Council English Committee's Drama Sub-Committee, held at Lady Margaret Hall, Oxford

(1974), Occasional Bulletin from the Subject Committees: *Examinations in Drama*, report of a working party of the Schools Council English Committee's Sub-Committee on Drama

(1981), *The Practical Curriculum* (March)

Seely, J. (1980), *In Role*, Oxford University Press

Slade, P. (1954), *Child Drama*, University of London Press

Spolin, V. (1973), *Improvisation for the Theatre*, North Western University Press

Standing Conference on Young People's Theatre (SCYPT) Journal (1980), no. 5

Taylor, J. L., and Walford, R. (1972), *Simulation in the Classroom*, Penguin Education

Terkel, S. (1970), *Hard times*, New York, Pantheon

Wagner, B. J. (1977), *Dorothy Heathcote: Drama as a Learning Medium*, Hutchinson

Walker, A. (1973), 'Everyday use', in *In Love and Trouble: Stories of Black Women*, New York: Harvest/Harcourt Brace Jovanovich

Warnock, M. (1977), *Schools of Thought*, Faber & Faber

Way, B. (1967), *Development Through Drama*, Longman

Willett, J. (1977), *The Theatre of Bertolt Brecht*, Eyre Methuen

Witkin, R. (1974), *The Intelligence of Feeling*, Heinemann

Wright, N. (1980), 'From the universal to the particular', in K. Robinson (ed.), *Exploring Theatre and Education*, Heinemann, 1980

Young, M. F. D. (1971), *Knowledge and Control*, Collier-Macmillan

Index